Michael M. Dediu

<u>2017</u>: World Top Events, But Many Little Known

A chronological and photographic documentary

DERC Publishing House

Tewksbury (Boston), Massachusetts, U. S. A.

Published and printed in the
United States of America
On the Great Seal of the United States are included:
E Pluribus Unum (Out of many, one)
Annuit Coeptis (He has approved of the undertakings)
Novus Ordo Seclorum (New order of the ages)

Library of Congress Control Number: 2018901792

Dediu, Michael M.

2017: World Top Events, But Many Little Known
A chronological and photographic documentary

ISBN-13: 978-1-939757630

Preface

Having in mind the quotes of Aristotle (384 BC – 322 BC) "Everybody, by nature, desires knowledge", and of Benjamin Franklin (1706 – 1790) "An investment in knowledge pays the best interest", we decided to present this book about the historical year 2017, so full of important events, but many so little known.

This book also proves another fundamental truth, first stated about 2,500 years ago by the illustrious pre-Socratic Greek philosopher Heraclitus of Ephesus (c 535 BC – c 475 BC, aged c 60): "The only constant is change."

We used information from 12 "Dediu Newsletters", in a chronological order, which include the most relevant news, in a balanced approach, usually directly from the source, not transformed by commentators, to help the general public to better understand the realities around us, which realities are sometimes not so pleasant, but always significant. We also included several nice photos.

It is very essential to inform the general public of this generation (and also of the future generations) about the many significant events and comments, which took place in this momentous year 2017. The more people know about what it happened, the better are chances that the severe problems, which need to be solved, will find the right and peaceful solutions.

Being well informed is a sine qua non requirement for everybody, in order to make the right decisions for the future.

The more you read, the more you'll love it! I want to thank my wife Sophia for her photo assistance.

This year 2017 will change many things, and any reader, no matter from what part of the world, will definitely find, in this book of general interest, numerous useful information, which will help them to better understand current events, and prepare them for a better future.

Michael M. Dediu, Ph. D.

Tewksbury (Boston), U. S. A., 12 February 2018

Michael M. Dediu is also the author of these books (which can be found on Amazon.com):

1. Aphorisms and quotations – with examples and explanations
2. Axioms, aphorisms and quotations – with examples and explanations
3. 100 Great Personalities and their Quotations
4. Professor Petre P. Teodorescu – A Great Mathematician and Engineer
5. Professor Ioan Goia – A Dedicated Engineering Professor
6. Venice (Venezia) – a new perspective. A short presentation with photographs
7. La Serenissima (Venice) - a new photographic perspective. A short presentation with many photos
8. Grand Canal – Venice. A new photographic viewpoint. A short presentation with many photos
9. Piazza San Marco – Venice. A different photographic view. A short presentation with many photos
10. Roma (Rome) - La Città Eterna. A new photographic view. A short presentation with many photos
11. Why is Rome so Fascinating? A short presentation with many photos
12. Rome, Boston and Helsinki. A short photographic presentation
13. Rome and Tokyo – two captivating cities. A short photographic presentation
14. Beautiful Places on Earth – A new photographic presentation
15. From Niagara Falls to Mount Fuji via Rome - A novel photographic presentation
16. From the USA and Canada to Italy and Japan - A fresh photographic presentation
17. Paris – Why So Many Call This City Mon Amour - A lovely photographic presentation
18. The City of Light – Paris (La Ville-Lumière) - A kaleidoscopic photographic presentation
19. Paris (Lutetia Parisiorum) – the romance capital of the world - A kaleidoscopic photographic view
20. Paris and Tokyo – a joyful photographic presentation. With a preamble about the Universe

21. From USA to Japan via Canada – A cheerful photographic documentary

22. 200 Wonderful Places, In The Last 50 Years – A personal photographic documentary

23. Must see places in USA and Japan - A kaleidoscopic photographic documentary

24. Grandeurs of the World - A kaleidoscopic photographic documentary

25. Corneliu Leu – writer on the same wavelength as Mark Twain. An American viewpoint

26. From Berkeley to Pompeii via Rome – A kaleidoscopic photographic documentary

27. From America to Europe via Japan - A kaleidoscopic photographic documentary

28. Discover America and Japan - A photographic documentary

29. J. R. Lucas – philosopher on a creative parallel with Plato, An American viewpoint

30. From America to Switzerland via France - A photographic documentary

31. From Bretton Woods to New York via Cape Cod - A photographic documentary

32. Splendid Places on the Atlantic Coast of the U. S. A. - A photographic documentary

33. Fourteen nice Cities on three Continents - A photographic documentary

34. 17 Picturesque Cities on the World Map - A photographic documentary

35. Unforgettable Places from Four Continents including Trump buildings - A photographic documentary

36. Dediu Newsletter, Volume 1, Number 1, 6 December 2016 – Monthly news, review, comments and suggestions for a better and wiser world

37. Dediu Newsletter, Volume 1, Number 2, 6 January 2017 (available at www.derc.com).

38. Dediu Newsletter, Volume 1, Number 3, 6 February 2017 (available at www.derc.com).

39. London and Greenwich, A photographic documentary

40. Dediu Newsletter, Volume 1, Number 4, 6 March 2017 (available also at www.derc.com).

41. Dediu Newsletter, Volume 1, Number 5, 6 April 2017 (available also at www.derc.com).

42. Dediu Newsletter, Volume 1, Number 6, 6 May 2017 (available also at www.derc.com).

43. Dediu Newsletter, Volume 1, Number 7, 6 June 2017 (available also at www.derc.com).

44. London, Oxford and Cambridge, A photographic documentary

45. Dediu Newsletter, Volume 1, Number 8, 6 July 2017 (available also at www.derc.com).

46. Dediu Newsletter, Volume 1, Number 9, 6 August 2017 (available also at www.derc.com).

47. Dediu Newsletter, Volume 1, Number 10, 6 September 2017 (available also at www.derc.com).

48. Three Great Professors: President Woodrow Wilson, Historian Germán Arciniegas, Mathematician Gheorghe Vrănceanu, A chronological and photographic documentary

49. Dediu Newsletter, Volume 1, Number 11, 6 October 2017 (available also at www.derc.com).

50. Dediu Newsletter, Volume 1, Number 12, 6 November 2017 (available also at www.derc.com).

51. Dediu Newsletter, Volume 2, Number 1 (13), 6 December 2017 (available also at www.derc.com).

52. Two Great Leaders: Augustus and George Washington, A chronological and photographic documentary

53. Dediu Newsletter, Volume 2, Number 2 (14), 6 January 2018 (available also at www.derc.com).

54. Newton, Benjamin Franklin, and Gauss, A chronological and photographic documentary

55. Dediu Newsletter, Volume 2, Number 3 (15), 6 February 2018 (available also at www.derc.com).

Michael M. Dediu is the editor of these books (also on Amazon.com):

1. Sophia Dediu: The life and its torrents – Ana. In Europe around 1920
2. Proceedings of the 4th International Conference "Advanced Composite Materials Engineering" COMAT 2012
3. Adolf Shvedchikov: I am an eternal child of spring – poems in English, Italian, French, German, Spanish and Russian
4. Adolf Shvedchikov: Life's Enigma – poems in English, Italian and Russian
5. Adolf Shvedchikov: Everyone wants to be HAPPY – poems in English, Spanish and Russian
6. Adolf Shvedchikov: My Life, My Love – poems in English, Italian and Russian
7. Adolf Shvedchikov: I am the gardener of love – poems in English and Russian
8. Adolf Shvedchikov: Amaretta di Saronno – poems in English and Russian
9. Adolf Shvedchikov: A Russian Rediscovers America
10. Adolf Shvedchikov: Parade of Life - poems in English and Russian
11. Adolf Shvedchikov: Overcoming Sorrow - poems in English and Russian
12. Sophia Dediu: Sophia meets Japan
13. Corneliu Leu: Roosevelt, Churchill, Stalin and Hitler: Their surprising role in Eastern Europe in 1944
14. Proceedings of the 5th International Conference "Computational Mechanics and Virtual Engineering" COMEC 2013
15. Georgeta Simion – Potanga: Beyond Imagination: A Thought-provoking novel inspired from mid-20th century events
16. Ana Dediu: The poetry of my life in Europe and The USA
17. Ana Dediu: The Four Graces
18. Proceedings of the 5th International Conference "Advanced Composite Materials Engineering" COMAT 2014
19. Sophia Dediu: Chocolate Cook Book: Is there such a thing as too much chocolate?

20. Sorin Vlase: Mechanical Identifiability in Automotive Engineering

21. Gabriel Dima: The Evolution of the Aerostructures – Concept and Technologies

22. Proceedings of the 6th International Conference "Computational Mechanics and Virtual Engineering" COMEC 2015

23. Sophia Dediu: Cook Book 1 A-B-C Common sense cooking

24. Sophia Dediu: Dim Sum Spring Festival

25. Ana Dediu & Sophia Dediu: Europe in 1985 - A chronological and photographic documentary

Table of Contents

Chapter 1. January 2017

From 1 January 2017 onwards, Switzerland has regained the status of "Associated Country" for the entire EU Framework Program "Horizon 2020".

On the 1st of January 2017, following a terrorist attack in Istanbul, Russian President Vladimir Putin (born 7 Oct 1952, now 64.2, divorced, 2 children) expressed condolences to President of the Republic of Turkey Recep Tayyip Erdogan (born 26 Feb 1954, now 62.8, married, 4 children) on the deaths of Turkish citizens and those of a number of other countries. "Our common duty is to decisively strike back against the terrorist aggression," the Russian President stressed in his message of condolences. President Putin confirmed that Russia has always been and will always remain Turkey's reliable partner in fighting terrorism.

The 3rd of January 2017 was the opening day of the 115th Congress, with Paul Ryan (born 29 Jan 1970, now 46.9) as the Speaker of the United States House of Representatives.

On 3 Jan 2017, President-elect Trump (born 14 June 1946, 70.5) tweeted: "With all that Congress has to work on, do they really have to make the weakening of the Independent Ethics Watchdog, as unfair as it may be, their number one act and priority. Focus on tax reform, healthcare and so many other things of far greater importance!" Less than two hours after this, House Republicans cancelled plans to reduce the Office of Congressional Ethics.

On 3 January 2017, Finland has started a major experiment: It is giving 2,000 citizens a "universal basic income" of €560 a month, with funds that keep rolling whether participants work or not. The program is hoped to cut government red tape, reduce poverty and boost employment, and could be expanded to include all adult Finns, if successful.

On 4 Jan 2017, Turkey's parliament has voted to extend the government's state of emergency powers for three months following the New Year's nightclub attack, claimed by Islamic State. At least

39 people, most of them foreign tourists, were shot dead early on Sunday 1 Jan 2017 morning by a lone gunman, who remains at large. The country is struggling to contain terrorist threats with depleted law enforcement ranks, in the wake of last year's failed coup.

Italy, Venezia: Il Campanile and Libreria Sansoviniana (left), Palazzo Ducale (center), Ponte della Paglia (right).

It is well known that sunlight allows us to make vitamin D, credited with healthier living, but a surprise research finding could reveal another powerful benefit of getting some Sun. Georgetown University Medical Center researchers have found that sunlight, through a mechanism separate than vitamin D production, energizes T cells that play a central role in human immunity. Their findings, published in Scientific Reports, suggest how the skin, the body's largest organ, stays alert to the many microbes that can nest there. They specifically found that low levels of blue light, found in Sun rays, makes T cells move faster — marking the first reported human cell responding to sunlight by speeding its pace. This research shows that sunlight directly activates key immune cells, by increasing their movement.

Eldercare robots are coming closer to senior living.

Soon it will be common for senior living residents and their caregivers to be assisted by robots, and sensors embedded throughout living spaces will be an integral part of healthcare.

6 Jan 2017: Dr. Rand Paul (born 7 Jan 1963, now 54, physician) Begins Second Term in the U.S. Senate

"We have our best chance in years to give you a government that defends your liberties and gets out of your way.

On Wednesday (4 Jan. 2017), I urged my colleagues to put a stop to Washington's runaway spending and pass a balanced budget. Right after Congress convened, I reintroduced my Federal Reserve Transparency Act, widely known as the "Audit the Fed" bill, to prevent the Federal Reserve from concealing vital information on its operations from Congress. Eight cosponsors joined me on the legislation.

On Wednesday (4 Jan. 2017), I reintroduced the "Regulations from the Executive in Need of Scrutiny" (REINS) Act as one of the first bills filed in the 115th Congress (S. 21). Twenty-six of my Senate colleagues joined me on the legislation as cosponsors. The REINS Act would rein in unelected federal bureaucrats by requiring that Congress affirmatively approve every new "major rule" proposed by the Executive Branch before it can be enforced on the American people.

Increasingly, regulatory agencies are wreaking havoc on freedom and our economy by imposing rules that carry the force of law, but lack approval by the people's representatives. Just ask Kentuckians about what the EPA's war on coal has cost our state! REINS is an important first step toward increasing accountability, oversight, and transparency in Washington, and it's one of the best ways President-elect Trump and the new Republican Congress can show we're responding to the American people's demand for change.

Replacing the current healthcare system is a priority.

I called for legislators to respect the American people's hard work and the Constitution's separation of powers.

I urged the Republican Party to get serious about enacting real tax cuts.

I noted that the "greatest security challenge facing the next president is the national debt. The United States owes nearly $20 trillion, not counting the nearly $50 trillion entitlement debt. The time approaches when America will no longer be able to manage its debt and fund national defense."

Ignoring the Constitution's separation of powers has fueled this skyrocketing debt, and straying from the Founders' vision also endangers our troops and country, through a reckless foreign policy.

If the Constitution isn't adhered to as the Founding Fathers intended, the nation and American credibility abroad suffer.

Shortly before Christmas, I released a special "Festivus: Airing of Grievances for 2016" edition of my "Waste Report," which collected all 37 Reports from 2016 about wasteful spending, misplaced priorities, and bad management in the federal government. All told, this spending cost taxpayers nearly two billion dollars! "Highlights" include: over $300,000 on TVs that sat waiting on a renovation project, and turned out to be the wrong kind, and $6,000,000 to renovate a Fort Belvoir cafeteria that closed permanently months later."

On 6 January 2017, Chinese President Xi Jinping (born 15 June 1953, now 63.5), also general secretary of the Communist Party of China (CPC) Central Committee and chairman of the Central Military Commission, spoke at the 7th plenary session of the 18th Communist Party of China (CPC) Central Commission for Discipline Inspection (CCDI). Adhering to the values of Communists and improving one's political conscientiousness is essential.

Over the weekend (7 Jan 2017), Trump wrote that "having a good relationship with Russia is a good thing... We have enough problems around the world without yet another one."

Russian President Vladimir Putin expressed his condolences to the leaders of Israel and Egypt, over the death of people in terrorist attacks in Jerusalem, Israel (on 8 Jan 2017), and in El-Arish, Sinai, Egypt (on 9 Jan 2017 – Putin said: "What happened proves yet again that the international community needs to consolidate its efforts in countering international terrorism." He reaffirmed that Russia is ready to further step up cooperation with its Egyptian partners in fighting this global threat.)

On 10 Jan. 2017, President-elect Trump has named his son-in-law as a senior adviser, who will work with incoming Chief of staff Reince Priebus (44), and chief strategist Stephen Bannon (63), on Middle East issues and trade negotiations. He will not receive a salary while serving in the Trump administration, which could help alleviate legal problems stemming from federal anti-nepotism law.

On 10 January 2017, Dr. Newt Gingrich (born 17 June 1943, 73.5), former Speaker, provided important information in his speech at the Heritage Foundation. There are over 513,000 elected officials. Republicans have over 4,100 state legislators (the most in the 162-year history of the Republican Party). There are 33 Republican Governors, the most since 1922. In fact, in 25 states there's absolute Republican control of the executive and legislative branches. There are currently 52 Republican Senators and 247 Republican House Members. They have a staff of approximately 7,500 people (25 staff/politician). There is a Cabinet with the Vice-President and the heads of 15 executive agencies. There are over 4,000 presidential appointees. The Senior Executive Service has around 7,700 members. There are over 900 general officers in the military.

On 12 Jan 2017, Russian President Vladimir Putin had a telephone conversation with President of Turkey Recep Tayyip Erdogan, at the Turkish side's initiative. The two leaders focused on the situation in Syria.

13 Jan 2017: Dr. Rand Paul Votes against an Unbalanced Budget - We must not sacrifice our children and grandchildren's futures, as well as our own economic security, to keep feeding an insatiable debt beast. As I mentioned last week, S. Con. Res. 3, the Senate's budget resolution, adds $9.7 trillion to the national debt over the next 10 years without ever balancing.
Early Thursday morning, I released the following statement after I voted "No" on that legislation:

"As a physician, I cannot wait to repeal Obamacare and replace it with a health care system that relies on freedom to provide quality, comprehensive, and affordable care.

"But putting nearly $10 trillion more in debt on the American people's backs through a budget that never balances is not the way to get there. It is the exact opposite of the change Republicans promised, and I cannot support it, even as a placeholder.

"Kentucky sent me to the Senate to put an end to the out-of-control spending. Unfortunately, this new Congress has chosen to continue the status quo. Not only are we not cutting spending, but we are also proposing an increase at an exponential pace. There is no reason we cannot repeal Obamacare and pass a balanced budget at the same time."

Dr. Rand Paul Presents "Worldwide Waste"

"On Tuesday (10 Jan 2017), I released the first installment of my "Worldwide Waste" series, a special project of "The Waste Report." "The Waste Report" alerts taxpayers to egregious examples of waste within the U.S. government to help reform spending and keep legislators accountable to the people.

In 2015 alone, the U.S. government's foreign assistance programs, which have largely escaped close scrutiny, absorbed $48 B of taxpayers' money. This amount represents the average tax liability of 6.6 millions of Americans - about one-and-a-half times the population of Kentucky!"

On 15 January 2017, Chinese President Xi Jinping and his wife Peng Liyuan (54, singer) was received by Swiss President Doris Leuthard (53) and her husband Roland Hausin at the Swiss Federal Council in Bern. Chinese President Xi Jinping attended a welcome ceremony held by all members of the Swiss Federal Council in Bern, on the same day. Chinese President Xi Jinping spoke highly of the China-Switzerland partnership, saying it has become a paradigm of relations between countries of different sizes. In 2016, Switzerland became the first and only country to set up a strategic partnership with China featuring innovation.

On 15 Jan 2017, Swiss police said that they have arrested 32 pro-Tibet activists, who were protesting, in Bern's center, against a visit by Chinese President Xi Jinping. The 700 protesters were made up of Tibetans and Swiss nationals, and were detained for breaking restrictions set up by police in the capital, Bern.

17 Jan. 2017. Former New York City Mayor Rudy Giuliani (72) announced on "Fox and Friends" that he will be heading up a new cyber security committee for President-elect Donald Trump. Fox News reports.

On 17 Jan 2017, making the first appearance by a Chinese leader at the forum in Davos, Switzerland, President Xi Jinping said the world's most important task is to revive the global economy, and free trade: "Protectionism is like locking oneself in a dark room. No one will win a trade war."

On 17 Jan 2017, Vladimir Putin held talks with President of Moldova, Igor Dodon (born 18 Feb 1975, now 41.9, married, 3 children), in the Kremlin. The talks focused on prospects for bilateral trade, economic, cultural and humanitarian cooperation and current regional issues, primarily a settlement in Transnistria.

On 18 Jan 2017, Russian President Vladimir Putin had a telephone conversation with Federal Chancellor of the Federal Republic of Germany, Angela Merkel (born 17 July 1954, now 62.5), and President of the French Republic, Francois Hollande (62).

The discussion dealt with progress toward implementing the Minsk agreements, including the outcome of the Normandy format summit in Berlin on October 19, 2016. Dissatisfaction was expressed with the general situation surrounding the settlement of the Ukraine crisis. In particular, the deterioration of the situation along the contact line in Donbass was noted, as well as the inadequate results of the Contact Group's efforts.

There was an emphasis on the importance of stepping up joint efforts to de-escalate tensions in southeastern Ukraine and ensuring consistent implementation of the Minsk-2 provisions, including an "all for all" exchange of detained persons as soon as possible. It was agreed to give an additional impetus to the Normandy format activities. In this regard, plans are in place to hold a series of meetings at various levels in the near future.

President Putin briefed his colleagues on steps to implement the Russian-Turkish-Iranian agreements on a ceasefire in Syria, and to prepare a meeting with the representatives of Damascus and the opposition, to be held in Astana on January 23, 2017.

On 18 January 2017, in his final major speech in his post, U.S. Vice President Joe Biden (74) issued a "call to action" to Europe and the U.S. to defend the "liberal world order," decrying a growing impulse in the West toward "isolationism and protectionism." Biden also acknowledged at the World Economic Forum in Davos that he'll hold his post for only another 48 hours, and quipped: "Then I can start to say what I think."

U.S. budget deficit widened to $28 B for December 2016, double the deficit for December 2015, when the gap was $14 B. The total U.S. budget deficit for 2016 was $587 B.

On 20 January 2017 at noon, on the steps of the U. S. Capitol, in Washington, D.C., the 45th President of the United States of America, Donald J. Trump (age 70.5), was sworn in.
In his Inaugural Address, President Trump mentioned:
"We, the citizens of America, are now joined in a great national effort to rebuild our country, and to restore its promise for all of our people."

Monday 23 Jan 2017 was a busy first day for President Trump: withdrew from TPP, promised to renegotiate NAFTA, placed a hiring freeze on federal employees, discussed slashing business regulations by 75%, reinstated the Mexico City policy, and vowed to stop the seizure by China of South China Sea islands.

On 23 Jan 2017, Chinese President Xi Jinping, also general secretary of the Communist Party of China (CPC) Central Committee and chairman of the Central Military Commission (CMC), called on the military to improve its political awareness, push forward reform, and govern it according to law, to aid the building of a strong military. Xi underscored the importance of improving combat readiness through troop training. It must be ensured that the military upholds the authority of the CPC Central

Committee at all times and under any circumstances, and firmly follows the command of the CPC Central Committee and the CMC, Xi said. He demanded reform tasks be implemented, and the military's combat capability be enhanced through drills under battle conditions.

On 25 Jan 2017, President Trump signed executive orders on immigration, on limiting the U.S. intake of refugees, and on building a wall on the south border.

On 25 Jan 2017, Vladimir Putin met with King Abdullah II bin Al-Hussein (55) of the Hashemite Kingdom of Jordan, who came to Moscow on a working visit at the invitation of the Russian President. The discussion focused on current issues in Russian-Jordanian cooperation and prospects for expanding trade, economic and humanitarian ties, as well as on current international and regional issues.

On 25 Jan 2017, North Korea announced that is ready to test-fire an intercontinental ballistic missile "at any time, at any place," said Choe Kang Il, deputy director general for North American affairs at North Korea's foreign ministry. "Our measures to bolster our nuclear arsenal are all defensive in nature." The country has conducted a total of five nuclear tests, including two last year, but has never successfully launched an ICBM.

On 26 Jan 2017, the U.K. Prime Minister May (60) offered to help President Trump to prevent the West from being "eclipsed" by China, as the PM urged him not to avoid his "obligation" to lead the world. The U.K. Prime Minister also hopes he can be an economically - after Britain's separation from Europe. The pair will meet face-to-face on 27 Jan 2017, making the PM the first foreign leader to step into Trump's Oval Office.

On 26 Jan 2017 Mexican President Enrique Pena Nieto (50.5) cancelled his meeting with President Trump, after Trump formally announced plans to build a border wall. The U.S. President also slashed funding to so-called sanctuary cities in the start of a strategy to tighten immigration controls. Construction of the wall will begin within "months," according to Trump, stating Mexico would reimburse the U.S. for the cost "100%."

On 27 Jan 2017, President Trump and Prime Minister May had Opening Remarks at their meeting. President Trump: "we look forward to working closely with you as we strengthen our mutual ties in commerce, business and foreign affairs. Great days lie ahead for our two peoples and our two countries."
Prime Minister May: "the invitation is an indication of the strength and importance of the special relationship that exists between our two countries -- a relationship based on the bonds of history, of family, kinship and common interest. And in a further sign of the importance of that relationship, I have today been able to convey Her Majesty The Queen's (90.8) hope that President Trump and the First Lady would pay a state visit to the United Kingdom later this year. And I'm delighted that the President has accepted that invitation."

On 27 Jan 2017, The United States President Donald J. Trump and Mexican President Enrique Peña Nieto spoke by phone in the morning, for an hour. The call was mutually arranged by their teams. The two had a productive and constructive call regarding the bilateral relationship between the two countries, the current trade deficit the United States has with Mexico, the importance of the friendship between the two nations, and the need for the two nations to work together to stop drug cartels, drug trafficking, and illegal guns and arms sales.

In the 4th quarter of 2016, the US annualized GDP growth was 1.9%. The total government (federal, state and local) spending rose at a 1.2% annualized rate. On 27 Jan 2017, the US national debt was over $19.9 T = $61,543/citizen = $166,776/taxpayer = 106.32% of the GDP.

On Saturday, 28 Jan 2017, Russian President Vladimir Putin had a telephone conversation with US President Donald Trump. Vladimir Putin congratulated Donald Trump of America on taking office and wished him every success in his work.

During the conversation, both sides expressed their readiness to make active joint efforts to stabilize and develop Russia-US cooperation on a constructive, equitable and mutually beneficial basis.

Mr. Putin and Mr. Trump had a detailed discussion of pressing international issues, including the fight against terrorism, the situation in the Middle East, the Arab-Israeli conflict, strategic stability and non-proliferation, the situation with Iran's nuclear program, and the Korean Peninsula issue. The discussion also touched upon the main aspects of the Ukrainian crisis. The sides agreed to build up partner cooperation in these and other areas.

The two leaders emphasized that joining efforts in fighting the main threat – international terrorism – is a top priority. The presidents spoke out for establishing real coordination of actions between Russia and the USA aimed at defeating ISIS and other terrorists groups in Syria.

The sides stressed the importance of rebuilding mutually beneficial trade and economic ties between the two counties' business communities, which could give an additional impetus to progressive and sustainable development of bilateral relations.

Mr. Putin and Mr. Trump agreed to issue instructions to work out the possible date and venue for their meeting.

Donald Trump asked to convey his wishes of happiness and prosperity to the Russian people, saying that the American people have warm feelings towards Russia and its citizens.

Vladimir Putin, in turn, emphasized that the feeling is mutual, adding that for over two centuries Russia has supported the United States, was its ally during the two world wars, and now sees the United States as a major partner in fighting international terrorism.

The two leaders agreed to maintain regular personal contacts.

The conversation took place in a positive and constructive atmosphere.

Calling Iran a "destabilizing influence" in the Middle East, National Security Adviser Mike Flynn (58) has officially put Iran "on notice", and warned of new U.S. sanctions following the country's weekend ballistic missile test.

Research by Skidmore College exercise scientist Paul Arciero has found that a balanced, protein-pacing, low-calorie diet that includes intermittent fasting, not only achieves long-term weight loss, but also helps release toxins in the form of PCBs.

Research shows that people's diet and weight, along with other lifestyle habits, can prevent up to 80% of heart attacks and strokes.

Octobot, created by Harvard researchers, is the world's first entirely soft robot, which is also self-sufficient.

The solution of disputes is not lawsuits, but education and friendly discussions.

Geneva, Switzerland, on Quai du Général Guisan (1874-1960), going southeast, the entrance to Swissotel Metropole Geneva (1854, 5 floors).

.

Chapter 2. February 2017

On 2 Feb 2017, following the restricted attendance consultations, Vladimir Putin and Viktor Orban (53) held a joint news conference in Budapest, followed by talks involving members of the delegations. The talks were focused on economic cooperation between Russia and Hungary and specific steps to boost trade and investment.

On 3 Feb 2017, a U.S. District Judge blocked the ban imposed by President Trump's immigration order, and on 5 Feb 2017 further court filings took place from both the government and DOJ. On 5 Feb 2017 President Trump tweeted "If something happens, blame him and court system." Some U.S. tech companies also have filed an amicus brief opposing the restrictions.

On 3 Feb 2017, Belarus President Alexander Lukashenko (62.5) had a big conversation with the press, in which he disapproved some of the Russian actions. In connection with the recent statements made by Belarusian leaders, the Press Service of the President of Russia notes that Moscow prioritizes the tasks and objectives of continuing the integration processes. Moscow also emphasizes the continuing development of the Union State of Russia and Belarus.

On 4 Feb 2017 President Donald J. Trump spoke with Prime Minister Paolo Gentiloni (62) of Italy, who invited him at the G-7 Summit. President Trump agreed to attend the G-7 Summit in Taormina, Italy in May 2017, and said he looked forward to meeting with the Prime Minister at that time.

On 4 Feb 2017, President Donald J. Trump had a very good call with President Petro Poroshenko (51) of Ukraine to address a variety of topics, including Ukraine's long-running conflict with Russia. "We will work with Ukraine, Russia, and all other parties involved, to help them restore peace along the border," said President Trump.

On 5 Feb 2017, President Donald J. Trump and Prime Minister Bill English (55) of New Zealand spoke on the telephone. The two leaders affirmed the close friendship and bilateral partnership between the United States and New Zealand.

On 5 Feb 2017, President Donald J. Trump spoke with NATO Secretary General Jens Stoltenberg (57) about the United States' strong support for NATO. The leaders discussed how to encourage all NATO allies to meet their defense spending commitments. Additionally, the parties discussed the potential for a peaceful resolution of the conflict along the Ukrainian border.

According to the latest figures, only five allies (Estonia, Greece, Poland, the U.K. and U.S.) met or exceeded the required 2% of GDP defense spending benchmark in 2016.

On 7 Feb 2017, President Donald J. Trump spoke with Prime Minister Mariano Rajoy (61.9) of Spain to reaffirm the strong bilateral partnership across a range of mutual interests.

On 7 Feb 2017, President Donald J. Trump spoke by phone with President Recep Tayyip Erdoğan of Turkey about the close, long-standing relationship between the United States and Turkey and their shared commitment to combating terrorism in all its forms. President Trump reiterated U.S. support to Turkey as a strategic partner and NATO ally, and welcomed Turkey's contributions to the counter-ISIS campaign.

On 7 Feb 2017, Russian President Vladimir Putin had a telephone conversation with Federal Chancellor of Germany Angela Merkel. The discussion focused on the situation in southeastern Ukraine, which recently deteriorated due to Ukraine's provocative actions. The parties expressed serious concern over the escalating armed conflict, which has caused casualties, and significant destruction of the civil infrastructure and residential areas in several Donbass towns. Vladimir Putin drew Angela Merkel's attention to the data of the OSCE Special Monitoring Mission as well as statements by official Kiev representatives, which indicate attempts by the Ukrainian security forces to change the situation at the contact line in their favor by military means. It is becoming obvious that

Kiev officials are trying to sabotage the execution of the Minsk Agreements and use the Normandy format to conceal their destructive acts. President Putin and Chancellor Merkel spoke for restoring the ceasefire immediately, and supported the efforts of the OSCE Special Monitoring Mission in this context.

The parties agreed to intensify diplomatic efforts to assist with the peaceful resolution of the Ukrainian crisis. In particular, this includes contacts between foreign ministers and the leaders' aides, within the Normandy format in the earliest possible timeframe, and subsequent discussions of the situation at the top level.

On 8 Feb 2017, President Donald J. Trump provided a letter to President Xi Jinping of China, thanking President Xi for his congratulatory letter on the occasion of President Trump's inauguration, and wishing the Chinese people a happy Lantern Festival and prosperous Year of the Rooster. President Trump stated that he looks forward to working with President Xi to develop a constructive relationship that benefits both the United States and China.

A US Navy plane approached a Chinese military aircraft on Wednesday, 8 Feb 2017, in the airspace near Huangyan Island (my note: this is a shoal (highest point: South Rock, 1.8 m) located 220 km west of Philippines, 700 km southwest of Taiwan, and 800 km southeast of China, claimed by China, Taiwan and Philippines), one of China's islands in the South China Sea, an official close to China's Defense Ministry said on Friday, 10 Feb. The Chinese plane, which was conducting routine training in the region, reacted professionally and adhered to law. "We hope the US will take the big picture of Sino-US military relations into account, and take practical measures to remove the root cause of accidents between the two countries in air and on sea," the official added.
This was the first time US and Chinese military planes met in 2017. The last two incidents were on May 17, 2016, and June 7, 2016.

On 9 Feb 2017, President Donald J. Trump and President Xi Jinping of China had a lengthy telephone conversation on. The two leaders discussed numerous topics, and President Trump agreed, at the request of President Xi, to honor our "one China" policy. Representatives of the United States and China will engage in discussions and negotiations on various issues of mutual interest. The phone call between President Trump and President Xi was extremely cordial, and both leaders extended best wishes to the people of each other's countries. They also extended invitations to meet in their respective countries. President Trump and President Xi look forward to further talks, with very successful outcomes.

On 9 Feb 2017, President Trump spoke with President Ghani (67.7) of the Islamic Republic of Afghanistan, and emphasized the ongoing importance of the U.S.-Afghanistan Strategic Partnership, and his support for the National Unity Government.

On 9 Feb 2017, President Trump spoke with His Highness Sheikh Sabah Al-Ahmad Al-Jabir Al-Sabah (87.5), the Amir of Kuwait. The President reaffirmed the strong defense partnership between the United States and Kuwait, and expressed appreciation to Kuwait for hosting U.S. military personnel.

On 9 Feb 2017, President Trump spoke by telephone with His Highness Sheikh Tamim Bin Hamad Al-Thani (36.5), the Amir of Qatar. They reaffirmed the close defense cooperation between our two countries, and committed to strengthen efforts to defeat violent terrorists. Regarding the situation in Syria, they agreed on the importance of defeating ISIS, and establishing the conditions for a successful political transition.

On 9 Feb 2017, President Donald J. Trump spoke with Prime Minister Haider al-Abadi (65) of Iraq to underscore the support of the United States for the Iraqi people in our shared fight against the terrorist group the Islamic State of Iraq and Syria (ISIS). President Trump emphasized the buildup of the United States military.

On 9 Feb 2017, Vladimir Putin had a telephone conversation with President of Turkey Recep Tayyip Erdogan. The two presidents continued their exchange of views on key aspects of the Syrian crisis in the context of the joint fight against international terrorism.

On 10 Feb 2017, President Donald J. Trump and Prime Minister Shinzo Abe (62.4) of Japan held their first official meeting in Washington D.C., and affirmed their strong determination to further strengthen the U.S.-Japan Alliance and economic relationship.

On 10 Feb 2017, Russian President Vladimir Putin met with President of Slovenia Borut Pahor (53). The agenda covered the full range of bilateral relations.

On 10 Feb 2017, Russian President Vladimir Putin congratulated King Felipe VI (49) of Spain on the 40th anniversary of the exchange of letters on establishing diplomatic relations between the two countries.

11 Feb 2017. President Donald J. Trump spoke with President Juan Manuel Santos (65) of Colombia over the weekend (11 Feb) to underscore the importance of continuing the long history of cooperation with Colombia, one of our strongest allies in the Western Hemisphere.

On 12 Feb 2017, President Donald J. Trump spoke today with President Pedro Pablo Kuczynski (78) of Peru, to reinforce the strong bilateral ties that exist between the United States and Peru.

On 12 Feb 2017, Vladimir Putin sent a message of congratulations to Frank-Walter Steinmeier (61) on being elected President of the Federal Republic of Germany

On 12 Feb 2017, Russian President Vladimir Putin congratulated Gurbanguly Berdimuhamedov (59.5) on his victory in Turkmenistan's presidential election.

On 13 Feb 2017, President Donald J. Trump and Prime Minister Justin Trudeau (45) held their first official meeting in Washington, D.C. and affirmed their longstanding commitment to close cooperation in addressing both the challenges facing our two countries, and problems around the world. No two countries share deeper or broader relations than Canada and the United States.

On 13 Feb 2017, the Treasury Department's Office of Foreign Asset Control -- OFAC -- labeled the Venezuelan Vice President as a specially designated narcotics trafficker, under the Kingpin Act.

On 13 Feb 2017, National Security Adviser Michael Flynn (Democrat) has resigned, apologizing to VP Mike Pence (57.5) for misleading him. Retired Army Lt. Gen. Keith Kellogg (Republican, 72.7) has been named as acting national security adviser in his stead.

On 15 Feb 2017, President Trump met at the White House with Prime Minister Netanyahu (67) of Israel.

On 15 Feb 2017, President Donald J. Trump Congratulates President-Elect Frank-Walter Steinmeier of Germany.

On 16 Feb 2017, Vladimir Putin met at the Kremlin with President of Uruguay Tabare Vazquez (77, physician).

On 16 Feb 2017, Syrian government calls on Turkey to withdraw its troops from Syria and close Turkish-Syrian border to the flow of terrorists. "Turkey should withdraw its troops from the territory of Syria," said Bashar al-Ja'afari, head of the Syrian government delegation at the peace talks in Astana, Kazakhstan, on Thursday, 16 Feb.

On 17 Feb 2017, President Xi Jinping has called for all Chinese, whether at home or abroad, to unite toward achieving the great rejuvenation of the Chinese nation. Xi made the remarks in a written instruction delivered at a national meeting on overseas Chinese affairs held in Beijing Friday, 17 Feb. It has been a key task for the Communist Party of China (CPC) and the state to encourage overseas Chinese, as well as returned Chinese, and their relatives to play a positive role in realizing the great revival of the Chinese nation, said Xi, who is also general secretary of the CPC Central Committee.

On 17 Feb 2017, Vladimir Putin took part in an annual expanded meeting of the Federal Security Service (FSB) Board to discuss the FSB's results for 2016 and the priority tasks for ensuring Russia's national security. The global situation has not become any more stable or better over the past year. On the contrary, many existing threats and challenges have only become more acute.

Military-political and economic rivalry between global and regional policy makers and between individual countries has increased. We see bloody conflicts continue in a number of countries in the Middle East, Asia, and Africa. International terrorist groups, essentially terrorist armies, receiving tacit and sometimes even open support from some countries, take active part in these conflicts.

At the NATO summit last July in Warsaw, Russia was declared the main threat to the alliance for the first time since 1989, and NATO officially proclaimed containing Russia its new mission. It is with this aim that NATO continues its expansion. This expansion was already underway earlier, but now they believe they have more serious reasons for doing so. They have stepped up the deployment of strategic and conventional arms beyond the national borders of the principal NATO member states. They are provoking us constantly and are trying to draw us into confrontation. We see continued attempts to interfere in our internal affairs in a bid to destabilize the social and political situation in Russia itself.

We also see the recent serious flare-up in southeast Ukraine. This escalation pursues the clear aim of preventing the Minsk Agreements from going ahead. The current Ukrainian authorities are obviously not seeking a peaceful solution to this very complex problem and have decided to opt for the use of force instead. What is more, they speak openly about organizing sabotage and terrorism, particularly in Russia. Obviously, this is a matter of great concern.

It is in our common interests to restore dialogue with the US intelligence services and with other NATO member countries. It is not our fault that these ties were broken off and are not developing.

On 18 Feb 2017, Chinese Xinhua reported about North Korea: "The Democratic People's Republic of Korea (DPRK) will "categorically reject" the post mortem conducted by Malaysia on its national, who died in Kuala Lumpur on Monday 13 Feb 2017, and demands the immediate transfer of the body, said the DPRK embassy in Malaysia on late Friday, 17 Feb."

"The Malaysian side forced the post mortem without our permission and witnessing, we will categorically reject the result of the post mortem conducted unilaterally excluding our attendance," DPRK's ambassador Kang Chol said in a statement delivered to the media outside the forensic department of Hospital Kuala Lumpur.

The victim, whom the Malaysian authorities claimed as Kim Jong Nam (45.8), the half-brother of the DPRK top leader Kim Jong Un (35, at 16 attended school in Switzerland for 2 years), was murdered in Kuala Lumpur on Monday.

On 20 Feb 2017, Lieutenant General H. R. McMaster (54.5) has been named as President Trump's new national security adviser, while retired Army Lt. Gen. Keith Kellogg, who had been his acting adviser, will now serve as the National Security Council chief of staff.

On 21 Feb 2017, Nobel laureate Chen Ning Yang (who studied in 1946 with Edward Teller at the University of Chicago, and was an assistant there to Enrico Fermi, then he was Professor at the Institute for Advanced Study in Princeton, and then at Stony Brook University), and Turing Award winner Andrew Yao Qizhi (who studied at Harvard University, then was Professor at Stanford University and Princeton University) have become Chinese citizens and officially joined the Chinese Academy of Sciences as academicians—the highest academic title in China, the academy's faculty office said. They are the first overseas scientists to relinquish their US citizenship to join the official faculty of China's highest scientific research organization. Yang, 94, will join the mathematical physics department, while Yao, 70, will enter the information technology and science department.

On 23 Feb 2017, Austrian Chancellor Christian Kern (51) declared that Britain should be charged about €60 B when it leaves the European Union, becoming the first EU leader to put a value on the size of the U.K.'s Brexit bill.

On 24 Feb 2017, at 3:06 P.M., in the Oval Office, President Trump and President Pedro Pablo Kuczynski of Peru had a few remarks before bilateral meeting.

North Korea and Malaysia have banned each other's nationals from departing their countries, escalating more than a week of tit-for-tat retaliation, following an investigation into the killing of Kim Jong Nam, half-brother of the leader of North Korea.

28 Feb 2017: some of the remarks by President Trump at Signing of Waters of the United States (WOTUS) Executive Order: "The EPA's so-called "Waters of the United States" rule is one of the worst examples of federal regulation, and it has truly run amok, and is one of the rules most strongly opposed by farmers, ranchers and agricultural workers all across our land. It's prohibiting them from being allowed to do what they're supposed to be doing. It's been a disaster. The Clean Water Act says that the EPA can regulate "navigable waters" -- meaning waters that truly affect interstate commerce. But a few years ago, the EPA decided that "navigable waters" can mean nearly every puddle or every ditch on a farmer's land, or anyplace else that they decide. It was a massive power grab. The EPA's regulators were putting people out of jobs by the hundreds of thousands, and regulations and permits started threatening our wonderful small farmers and small businesses. They treated them horribly. Horribly. If you want to build a new home, for example, you have to worry about getting hit with a huge fine if you fill in as much as a puddle -- just a puddle -- on your lot. I've seen it. In fact, when it was first shown to me, I said, no, you're kidding aren't you? But they weren't kidding.
In one case in Wyoming, a rancher was fined $37,000 a day by the EPA for digging a small watering hole for his cattle. His land. These abuses were, and are, why such incredible opposition to this rule from the hundreds of organizations took place in all 50 states. It's a horrible, horrible rule. I've been hearing about it for years and years. With today's executive order, I'm directing the EPA to take action, paving the way for the elimination of this very destructive and horrible rule."

28 Feb 2017: President Donald Trump's first address to Congress. The President pledged to overhaul the immigration system, improve jobs and wages for Americans, and promised "massive" tax relief to the middle class, and tax cuts for companies. He also plans to ask Congress for $1T in infrastructure investment.

Researchers at Mount Sinai Health System have discovered an algorithm to predict whether blood cancer patients, who received a bone marrow transplant, will develop graft-versus-host disease, a common and often lethal complication.

The risk of high blood pressure begins to climb when men turn 45.

New research in Switzerland shows good results in purifying blood with magnetism.

A new survey shows that young Swiss are the bests in Mathematics in Europe

The Rainbow Bridge between Canada (left) and USA (right), crosses Niagara River, 500 m north-west from the American Falls, opened 1941, longest span 298 m, seen from the Prospect Point Observation Tower (70 m north of the American Falls).

Chapter 3. March 2017

On 2 March 2017, Russian President Vladimir Putin congratulated the last President of the Soviet Union (1990-1991). Mikhail Gorbachev, president of the International Foundation for Socio-Economic and Political Studies, on his 86th birthday (2 March 1931).

5 March 2017. Chinese President Xi Jinping said Sunday, 5 March 2017, that China will stick to the all-round opening-up policy, and continue to liberalize and facilitate trade and investment.

On 6 March 2017, North Korea fired four ballistic missiles into nearby waters, three of which landed in Japan's exclusive economic zone.

On 6 March 2017, President Donald J. Trump spoke separately with Prime Minister Shinzo Abe of Japan, and Acting President Hwang Kyo-Ahn (59.9) of South Korea, to discuss North Korea's launch of ballistic missiles, in clear violation of multiple U.N. Security Council resolutions.

On 6 March 2017, Japan moved to the highest possible alert level, after North Korea fired four ballistic missiles. "This clearly shows North Korea has entered a new stage of threat," Prime Minister Shinzo Abe declared.

6 and 7 March 2017. The Turkish chief of the general staff, Army Gen. Hulusi Akar (65), invited US Marine Corps Gen., Joe Dunford (61), and Russian chief of the general staff, Army Gen. Valery Gerasimov (61), to a meeting in Antalya, Turkey, March 6-7, 2017, to discuss conditions in Syria, and the measures needed to protect each other's forces in the region. The three chiefs of defense and their staffs met at the Regnum Resort to describe conditions on the ground in Syria as each nation sees them, and to devise methods of deconflicting operations.

South Korea and the U.S. conduct their annual military drills and war games. Despite strong opposition from China, the U.S. has started to deploy the first elements of its Terminal High Altitude Area Defense (THAAD) anti-missile defense system in South Korea, after North Korea's recent test of four ballistic missiles.

China has repeatedly said that the Republic of Korea (ROK) and U.S. deployment of THAAD gravely undermined regional strategic balance, and the security interests of countries in the region, including China, and runs counter to peace and stability in the Korean Peninsula. THAAD is designed to intercept incoming missiles at an altitude of 40-150 km. Its X-band radar can peer deep into Chinese and Russian territories.

South Korea wants swarming drones equipped with explosives to attack multiple targets.

Harris Corp. is supplying a next-generation, VoIP communication system to support Taiwan's military air defense system, officials announced during World ATM Congress in Madrid.

On 7 March 2017, China was calling for North Korea to stop its nuclear and missile tests, and for South Korea and the U.S. to cease joint military drills. The moves are causing tension to increase.

In Dubai, United Arab Emirates, Poly Technologies from Beijing, China, is showing off The Silent Hunter, one of the world's most powerful laser weapons. It claims an output of at least 50-70 kilowatts, which would make it more powerful than the 33-kilowatt laser weapon systems (LaWS) currently deployed on the USS Ponce, ZeroHedge reports. The Chinese laser weapon is probably based on the Low Altitude Guard. That's enough to knock out automobiles by burning out their engines from over 1.6 km away.

On 7 March 2017, Chinese President Xi Jinping said that the northeastern province of Liaoning must depend on the real economy to realize rejuvenation, stressing the leading role of state-owned companies.

China is making a new-generation manned spaceship, which rivals that of world-leading space powers, a space mission expert said. "Among the next generation of manned spaceships some foreign countries are developing, only the Orion spacecraft of the US can carry out a moon landing mission," Zhang Bainan, a spaceship engineer with China Aerospace Science and Technology Corp, told Science and Technology Daily on Tuesday, 7 March 2017. China is working on a new manned spaceship that can fly both in low earth orbit, as well as a moon landing mission, Zhang said. He added that the spacecraft is recoverable and has a larger capacity than the new-generation manned spaceship of foreign countries, which can carry six people in low earth orbit and three to four in a moon landing mission. Last year, the re-entry module of the new spacecraft was put to the test aboard a Long March-7 rocket.

China first launched a man into space in 2003, 42 years after the former Soviet Union carried out the maiden manned space flight.

The country is projected to build a space station in 2020, and make a manned moon landing in 2030.

On 7 March 2017, Vladimir Putin had a telephone conversation with Prime Minister of Hungary Viktor Orban at the initiative of the Hungarian side. The presidents expressed satisfaction with the European Commission's decision to lift obstacles that prevented Rosatom from contributing to the construction of two reactors for the Paks nuclear power plant in Hungary.

9 March 2017. The Chengdu J-20, China's independently developed fourth-generation stealth fighter has entered service with the People's Liberation Army Air Force (PLAAF), as revealed by the military channel of China Central Television (CCTV) on March 9, 2017.

On 9 March 2017, Vladimir Putin met with Minister of Foreign Affairs and Vice Chancellor of Germany Sigmar Gabriel (57). The current state of bilateral relations, and prospects for their development, was the subject of discussion.

On 9 March 2017, Vladimir Putin met at the Kremlin with Prime Minister of Israel, Benjamin Netanyahu, who is in Russia on a brief working visit. Mr. Putin and Mr. Netanyahu discussed the situation in the Middle East, in particular in Syria, in the context of joint efforts to combat international terrorism, and examined the main areas of bilateral cooperation.

On 9 March 2017, the Moldovan leaders of the government and parliament (both of Romanian origin, speaking Romanian; the President of Moldova is of Russian origin, speaking Russian) presented a diplomatic démarche to the Russian ambassador in Chişinău, regarding numerous abuses and harassments by the Russian authorities, against Moldovan officials visiting Russia. They asked the Russian government to stop these abuses, and they will not anymore visit Russia, until they receive a satisfactory response.

9 March 2017. Iran's Tasnim news agency reported that the Islamic Revolution Guards Corps (IRGC) had carried out an anti-ship missile test. When it was unveiled in May 2014, the Hormuz-2 appeared to be an active radar-guided variant of Iran's Khalij Fars ASBM, while the Hormuz-1 was said to be a passive radar-guided variant.

Iran has imposed sanctions on 15 American companies for alleged human rights violations, and cooperating with Israel, just days after the U.S. imposed penalties on 30 foreign entities for transferring sensitive technology to Tehran. The US firms include United Technologies, ITT Corp., Raytheon, Re/Max Real Estate, Oshkosh and Elbit Systems.

On 10 March 2017, Vladimir Putin met with the President of Turkey, Recep Tayyip Erdogan, in the Kremlin. The President of Turkey has come to Russia for the sixth meeting of the High-Level Russian-Turkish Cooperation Council.

10 March 2017. Russian warplanes launched 452 strikes against Islamic State (IS) terrorists in Syria in the past week (6-10 March 2017), as the government troops continued their advance in the north and east of the war-torn country, the Russian military said

Friday, 10 March 2017. "Over 600 militants, 16 infantry fighting vehicles, 41 pickup trucks with large caliber machine-guns and more than 30 other vehicles have been eliminated," Col. Gen. Sergei Rudskoy, chief of the Russian General Staff Main Operational Directorate, said at a news briefing. He said the Syrian troops liberated 92 terrorists' settlements on an area of 479 square km in the eastern part of Aleppo province, in the last seven days, reaching the bank of the Euphrates River for the first time in the last four years. After taking control of the ancient city of Palmyra, the Syrian government troops continued their offensive to the east of the city, capturing dominant heights, and extend the security zone to the north and south, Rudskoy said. Russian and Syrian sappers had started a mine clearing operation at historical monuments of Aleppo, he added.

Russia held the second place in the world, in 2016, in terms of military exports, which came to more than $15 billions, compared with $14.5 billions in 2015. The Stockholm International Peace Research Institute (SIPRI) estimates that Russia accounts for 23% of global arms exports. The United States is substantially ahead, with 33%, then China, with 6.2%, France, with 6%, and Germany, with 5.6%. Russia military exports to 52 countries, and the defense industry's export portfolio remains at the $50-billions level.

On 11 March 2017, Turkish President Erdogan accused the Dutch government of Nazism, and threatened to retaliate in the "harshest ways." He made the comments after two Turkish politicians were denied entry into the country, to take part in a constitutional referendum campaign rally. "If Europe continues this way, no European in any part of the world can walk safely on the streets," President Erdogan declared in his latest salvo in a row over campaigning by Turkish politicians in Europe.

On 11 March 2017, U.S. space agency NASA has successfully located India's first lunar spacecraft Chandrayaan-1 that lost contact with ground controllers on Earth eight years ago. NASA found the spacecraft by using a new technological application of ground-based interplanetary radar, and said it's still circling some 200 kilometers above the lunar surface.

This new technique also discovered an active spacecraft orbiting the moon, NASA's Lunar Reconnaissance Orbiter (LRO).
LRO was launched on June 18, 2009, while India's Chandrayaan-1 was launched on October 22, 2008.

13 March 2017. The federal board overseeing Puerto Rico's finances will meet on 13 March 2017, in New York, where it must decide on a plan for ending its chronic deficits. The island hopes to restructure more than $110 B of debt and pension obligations, but it must first produce a credible fiscal plan. Last week, the board told Gov. Ricardo A. Rossello (38) his proposal was unrealistic, and asked him to make revisions.

Japan, north-west of the Sendai Station (1887), on Ekimae Dori, the restaurant Rigoletto, named after the famous opera with the same name, by Giuseppe Verdi (1813 – 1901), who wrote 37 operas, Rigoletto being the 17th, with the premiere at Teatro La Fenice, Venezia, on 11 March 1851.

On 14 March 2017, at the White House, President Donald J. Trump and Saudi Deputy Crown Prince, Mohammed bin Salman (31.5), reaffirmed their support for a strong, broad, and enduring strategic partnership, based on a shared interest and commitment to the stability and prosperity of the Middle East region.

14 March 2017. Pi Day is celebrated on March 14th around the world. Pi (Greek letter "π") is the symbol used in mathematics to represent a constant — the ratio of the circumference of a circle to its diameter — which is approximately 3.14159. Pi has been calculated to over one trillion digits beyond its decimal point. As an irrational and transcendental number, the digits beyond its decimal point will continue infinitely, without repetition or pattern. Practically, only a handful of digits are needed for typical calculations. Pi and mathematics are permanently used in all disciplines, and they are a sine qua non requirement for doing research and innovation.

15 March 2017. Hours before it was to take effect, on 16 March 2017, President Trump's revised travel ban was put on hold on 15 March 2017 by a federal judge in Hawaii. "This ruling makes us look weak," Trump said, vowing to fight the "unprecedented judicial overreach... all the way to the Supreme Court." Following the second version of the ban, almost 70 tech companies backed away from their proposed legal suit, representing more than half of the original 127 signatories.

On 15 March 2017, Vladimir Putin met with President of Armenia, Serzh Sargsyan (62.6), who is in Russia on an official visit. The two presidents discussed key bilateral cooperation matters, and prospects for the development of integration cooperation in the Eurasian region.

16 March 2017. The White House. President Donald J. Trump met on 16 March 2017 with Taoiseach Enda Kenny (65.9) of Ireland, to discuss United States-Ireland economic and cultural ties, as part of the White House St. Patrick's Day celebration.

16 March 2017. Vladimir Putin met with Minister-President of the Federal Land of Bavaria, Horst Seehofer (67), who is in Moscow at the invitation of Moscow Mayor, Sergei Sobyanin (58).

16 March 2017. The U.S. debt ceiling limit expired on 16 March 2017, potentially setting up an intense political battle in

Congress. Treasury Secretary Steven Mnuchin (54) has encouraged Congress to raise the ceiling "at the first opportunity," while Senate Majority Leader Mitch McConnell (75) said on 14 March that Congress will "obviously" increase the limit. The current U.S. national debt is $19.4 T.

17 March 2017. President Trump welcomed German Chancellor Merkel (62.5) to the White House.

17 March 2017. Vladimir Putin met with President of Moldova, Igor Dodon (42), in the Kremlin. The two leaders discussed arrangements reached following top-level talks in January, economic cooperation, and topical regional issues.

On 18 March 2017, Vladimir Putin had a telephone conversation with President of Kazakhstan, Nursultan Nazarbayev (76.5).

20 March 2017. North Korea's latest missile test, on 20 March 2017, apparently exploded within seconds after liftoff. The failed launch comes after Pyongyang vowed to accelerate its missile programs, and to fight back against any U.S. move to broaden sanctions.

North Korea has carried out another test of a rocket engine that U.S. officials believe could be part of its program to develop an ICBM. It's the third such test in recent weeks.

On 21 March 2017, EU Enlargement Commissioner Johannes Hahn (59) told Bild that "with regard to the strict accession criteria, Turkey has been moving further and further away from the EU for some time."

On 24 March 2017, the United States congratulated the European Union on the sixtieth anniversary of the 1957 Treaties of Rome, and the founding of the European Economic Community. Our two continents share the same values and, above all, the same commitment to promote peace and prosperity through freedom, democracy, and the rule of law. Together we look forward to another sixty years and more of shared security and shared prosperity.

On 24 March 2017, Vladimir Putin met in Moscow with Marine Le Pen (48), leader of the French National Front Party.

The U.S. national debt is standing at nearly $20 trillion, and the government is set to owe a $295 billion interest payment just this year. One Senator said: "Our present, unsustainable course directly threatens our national security, and long-term stability. The interest on our debt today is roughly 7% of federal spending. By comparison, roughly 14% of our budget is spent on national defense."

Designed to counter medium-range missiles, the middle layer of Israel's three-tier missile shield, has become operational. David's Sling was developed by Israeli defense firm Rafael with American defense giant Raytheon. The system adds to the Iron Dome, which defends against short-range rockets, and Arrow 3, aimed at long-range ballistic missiles in the stratosphere.

On 25 March 2017, President Xi Jinping sent a congratulatory letter to the opening ceremony of the 2017 annual conference of the Boao Forum for Asia (a Chinese Davos, modeled after the world Economic Forum in Davos (Switzerland)), held in China's Hainan Province Saturday morning (Boao is a town on the central eastern coastal part of the island Hainan, in South China Sea, southwest of China, 800 km southwest of Hong Kong, 600 km southeast of Hanoi (Vietnam)).
Since its establishment 16 years ago, the Boao Forum for Asia has played an important role in building Asian consensus, promoting Asian cooperation and upgrading Asian influence, Xi noted.
The theme for this year's conference is "Globalization and Free Trade: The Asian Perspectives."

A committee of 63 aviation specialists from across China has agreed the C919 is technically ready for its maiden flight, Xinhua reports. China's first national passenger jet aims to challenge the dominance of Boeing's 737 and Airbus's A320, in the global commercial aviation market. COMAC has already received 570 orders for C919 planes.

On 26 March 2017, police detained hundreds of protesters across Russia, including opposition leader Alexei Navalny (40.6), after thousands took to the streets to demonstrate against corruption, and demand the resignation of Prime Minister Dmitry Medvedev (51.5). It was the biggest show of defiance since a 2011-2012 wave of demonstrations upset the Kremlin, and led to harsh new laws aimed at suppressing dissent.

On 27 March 2017, Chinese President Xi Jinping met with Nepali Prime Minister, Pushpa Kamal Dahal (62), in Beijing, and they agreed to cooperate more in jointly building the Belt and Road.

On 27 March 2017, China and Madagascar agreed to synergize development strategies under the framework of the Belt and Road Initiative, and ten major plans for China-Africa cooperation. The pledge came out of the talks between Chinese President Xi Jinping, and President of Madagascar Hery Rajaonarimampianina (58.3), in Beijing.

On 27 March 2017, in the Kremlin, Vladimir Putin met with Prime Minister of Serbia, Aleksandar Vucic (47). Bilateral relations were the main subject on the agenda, in particular, developing trade and investment cooperation. The two leaders also exchanged views on current international and regional issues.

On 27 March 2017, in New Zeeland, Chinese Premier Li Keqiang said that China and New Zealand will jointly establish an upgraded free trade area, with more open trade and investment, to promote bilateral trade cooperation and economic globalization.

On 28 March 2017, Vladimir Putin met with President of Iran, Hassan Rouhani (68.3), in the Kremlin. The two leaders discussed prospects for expanding trade, economic and investment ties, including in the context of implementing major joint projects in energy and transport infrastructure. They exchanged views on important current issues on the global and regional agenda.

On 28 March 2017, Vladimir Putin sent his greetings to participants in the League of Arab States' summit (22 countries: Algeria, Bahrein, Comoros, Djibouti, Egypt, Iraq, Jordan, Kuwait, Lebanon, Libya, Mauritania, Morocco, Oman, Palestine, Qatar, Saudi Arabia, Somalia, Sudan, Syria, Tunisia, United Arab Emirates and Yemen). "The Middle East and North Africa are going through tense and difficult times today. The conflicts in Syria, Iraq, Libya and Yemen remain heated, terrorism and extremism continue to escalate, social and economic problems are becoming increasingly acute. Undoubtedly, this makes the League of Arab States more needed than ever as a mechanism for multilateral dialogue and coordinating collective efforts."

On 30 March 2017, Vladimir Putin took part in the fourth international forum The Arctic: Territory of Dialogue, in Arkhangelsk. Also attended by the President of Finland, Sauli Niinistö (68.5), and the President of Iceland, Mr. Johannesson (48). The forum's theme this year is People and the Arctic. The participants are discussing ways to improve the quality of life in the Arctic, maintain its unique environmental potential, boost sustainable socioeconomic development of the Arctic regions, and strengthen international cooperation for these purposes.

Vladimir Putin had a meeting with President of Finland, Sauli Niinistö, on the sidelines of the international forum Arctic: Territory of Dialogue.

President of Russia Vladimir Putin: Mr. President, colleagues, friends, welcome to Arkhangelsk.

I would like to thank you once again for accepting our invitation. Your participation in these discussions on the Arctic's development is extremely important, because we are all Arctic countries, and this kind of open and free discussion creates an atmosphere of trust, and creates conditions for resolving the region's development issues.

Of course, we also have the opportunity today to discuss our bilateral relations. We are very happy to see you.

President of Finland Sauli Niinistö : "Thank you very much. It was with pleasure that we have come here. It is very important that you, Vladimir, support discussion and dialogue on the Arctic, which is a focus of attention now. Finland will soon take on the presidency in the Arctic Council, and all that we take away from here, from this forum, will help us in our further work.

There are also many bilateral issues that it would be useful to discuss. As always, I would be keen to know and hear your view of the world. Thank you very much for the invitation."

In Arkhangelsk (Russia), within the framework of the international forum Arctic: Territory of Dialogue, Vladimir Putin had a meeting with President of Iceland, Gudni Johannesson.

On 31 March 2017, China informs: U.S. President Donald Trump looks forward to meeting with Chinese President Xi Jinping to chart a way forward on the U.S.-China relationship, the White House said Thursday. The two leaders will meet at Mar-a-Lago, Florida on April 6-7 for their first meeting since Trump assumed office in January, China and the United States concurrently announced earlier Thursday. "The president looks forward to meeting with President Xi and exchanging views on each other's respective priorities, and to chart a way forward on a bilateral relationship between our two nations," White House spokesman Sean Spicer told a news briefing. They will discuss issues of mutual concern, including the Democratic People's Republic of Korea, trade, and regional security, he added. Spicer said the two sides reached agreement on the dates, locations and agendas of the Xi-Trump summit after several weeks of discussions. Asked about the U.S. goal for the meeting, Spicer said this will be an opportunity for Trump "to develop a relationship in person with President Xi."

Before his US trip, Xi will make a state visit to Finland from Tuesday to Thursday, which will be Xi's first visit to northern Europe as president.

Wang Chao, vice-foreign minister, said Xi will hold talks with Finnish President, Sauli Niinisto, and attend a ceremony for the signing of cooperative documents, a joint news conference, and a welcome banquet.

On 31 March 2017, a Foreign Ministry spokesperson said China is firmly opposed to any visit by the Dalai Lama (81.5) to the disputed border region between China and India.

"China is gravely concerned about this. Our stance on the eastern part of the China-India border is clear and consistent".

The Dalai Lama has long engaged in anti-China separatist activities, and has behaved disgracefully on the China-India border issue.

India understands the seriousness of the Dalai Lama issue and the sensitivity of the border disputes, he said, noting that India's invitation to the Dalai Lama for activities in the disputed border areas will gravely damage peace and stability of the border areas, as well as bilateral relations. China demands the Indian side meet its political commitments on Tibet-related issues and abide by the consensus reached by the two sides on border issues.

He urged India to refrain from taking actions that could further complicate the China-India border issue, and to not provide a platform for separatist activities of the Dalai Lama clique, in order to safeguard the healthy and stable development of bilateral ties.

"Maintaining a good relationship between the two big developing countries serves the interests of the two peoples. But China-India relations are based on certain principles". Similar incidents have happened in the past, and triggered opposition from China, resulting in harm to bilateral relations. "Therefore, we urge the Indian side to deliver its political commitments on this issue so that bilateral relations won't be hurt. Otherwise, it will also be detrimental to India," the spokesperson said.

It appears that China is working on hypersonic attack drones, and other hypersonic weapons, to be ready by 2040.

Hong Kong's electoral committee has hand-picked a resolutely pro-China candidate, Carrie Lam (59.8), to lead the city. This selection underscores China's growing political influence on the former British colony. In 2014, parts of the city were paralyzed when tens of thousands of protesters blocked major roads, for nearly three months, to demand China to allow full democracy.

University of California, Irvine, researchers have identified a specific mutation that allows melanoma tumor cells to remain undetected by the immune system.

Paris: statue of Pierre Corneille (1606 – 1684, poet and dramatist, the creator of French classical tragedy (Le Cid, Horace, Cinna, La Place royale), one of the three great 17th century French dramatists, along with Molière (1622 – 1673) and Racine (1639 – 1699)) and Paroisse Saint-Étienne-du-Mont (center, 510, 1222, 1328, 1492-1626) – a Catholic church, north-east of the Panthéon (right), with the tombs of Blaise Pascal (1623 – 1662, mathematician, physicist, philosopher, inventor and writer) and Jean-Baptiste Racine.

Chapter 4. April 2017

On 2 April, 2017, in an interview with the Financial Times, President Trump said he would discuss North Korea with Xi Jinping next weekend, during his first meeting with the Chinese President. "If they do [help us], that will be very good for China, and if they don't, it won't be good for anyone," he declared, adding that the U.S. is willing to take unilateral action against the nuclear regime.

3 April 2017. A suspect (suicide bomber) in the metro blast of 3 April 2017 (an unidentified device exploded at 2:40 PM in a train between the metro stations Tekhnologichesky Institut and Sennaya Ploshchad in St. Petersburg), which killed 11 people and injured 45, is a 22-year old Kyrgyz-born Russian citizen. Interfax news reports. No group has claimed responsibility for the deadly explosion, which Russia's National Antiterrorist Committee is investigating as a terrorist attack.

On 3 April 2017, Vladimir Putin met with President of Belarus, Alexander Lukashenko, in St Petersburg to discuss current issues of bilateral relations.

3 April 2017. The White House. President Donald J. Trump spoke with President Vladimir Putin (64.5) of the Russian Federation, to condemn today's attack in St. Petersburg. President Trump expressed his deepest condolences to the victims and their loved ones, and to the Russian people. President Trump offered the full support of the United States Government in responding to the attack, and bringing those responsible to justice. Both President Trump and President Putin agreed that terrorism must be decisively and quickly defeated.

4 April 2017. The Kremlin (about the same phone call presented above). Vladimir Putin had a telephone conversation with US President Donald Trump. US President Donald Trump offered his condolences to the families and friends of the victims of the heinous terrorist attack in the St Petersburg metro, and asked Vladimir Putin to convey his words of support to the Russian people. President Putin thanked his American colleague for the expression

of solidarity. The Presidents noted that terrorism is an evil that must be fought jointly, and agreed to continue their contacts.

On 4 April 2017. North Korea has fired a medium-range ballistic missile into the Sea of Japan. "The U.S. has spoken enough about North Korea. We have no further comment," Secretary of State Tillerson (65) declared. The launch comes a day ahead of the summit between Trump and China's Xi in Mar-a-Lago, where they will discuss dealing with North Korea's nuclear development program.

4 April 2017. In Syria's city of Khan Sheikhoun, in the northwestern province of Idlib, chemical weapons kill over 70 people.

5 April 2017. Russian Defense Ministry said on Wednesday, 5 April 2017, that the deadly gas contamination in Syria was caused by the explosion of chemical weapons produced and stored by the rebels, after Syrian aircraft bombed the area. Damascus has repeatedly denied possession of any chemical weapons.

6 April 2017. The U.S. Congress is divided over the missile strike at Syria on 6 April 2017 evening (7 April 2017 early morning in Syria), with some lawmakers questioning its constitutionality.
The U.S. military fired 59 Tomahawk cruise missiles (total cost over $100 M, which could buy over 300 good family houses in the U. S.), which were launched from U.S. destroyers USS Porter and USS Ross, in the Eastern Mediterranean Sea, at a Syrian military base, after a chemical attack in Syria's city of Khan Sheikhoun, in the northwestern province of Idlib, which killed at least 70 people, mostly civilians. The administration held the Syrian government led by President Bashar al-Assad (51) responsible for Tuesday's gas attack, even if some said that the terrorists were responsible.
The assault, ordered by U.S. President Donald Trump, was the first direct U.S. assault on the army of Syrian President Bashar al-Assad, since Syrian crisis began six years ago. Most Congress members were not notified of the military action, as they were preparing to leave Washington D.C., for a two-week Easter recess.

Reaction to the strike mostly followed a partisan line, as most Republican lawmakers endorsed the action, while most Democrats were opposed, on the grounds that he needed authorization of Congress for acts of war.

In the Republican camp there are many doubting the legality of this action, including Republican Senator Rand Paul (54) and House Representative Justin Amash (37).

Dr. Paul criticized Trump's order to strike Syria as unconstitutional. "The Constitution is very clear that war originates in the legislature," he told reporters on 7 April 2017. "You vote before you go to war, not after you go to war," Dr. Paul said.

Amash questioned the administration's justification in making the decision, saying such strikes are "act of war" that requires authorization from Congress.

"Airstrikes are an act of war. Atrocities in Syria cannot justify departure from Constitution, which vests in Congress power to commence war," he tweeted on 6 April 2017 night.

26 Nov 2008, Shinjuku Center Building (223 m, 54 fl, 1979, center), Mode Gakuen Cocoon Tower (204 m, 50 fl, 2008, center-right), Keio Plaza Hotel North Tower (180 m, 47 fl, 1971, right).

7 April 2017. Xinhua. Chinese President Xi (63.8) Jinping, who is firstly General Secretary of the Central Committee of the

Communist Party of China and Chairman of the Central Military Commission of the Communist Party of China, and his U.S. counterpart, Donald Trump (70.8), pledged to expand mutually beneficial cooperation, and manage differences on the basis of mutual respect.

The two leaders also agreed that their first meeting, held at the seaside Mar-a-Lago resort in the U.S. state of Florida, was "positive and fruitful." During their talks over the two days, Xi and Trump exchanged views on key areas of bilateral cooperation, as well as global and regional issues of common concern.

Xi said his first meeting with Trump bears unique significance to the development of China-U.S. ties.

He added that he and Trump, during the meeting, have also gained better understanding of each other, cemented their mutual trust, scored many major consensuses, and built up a good working relationship. The two sides need to further enhance their relations, so as to better serve the interests of the two countries and their peoples, and to promote world peace and prosperity, Xi said.

China and the United States are now each other's biggest trading partner, from which the two peoples benefit a lot, said Xi.

Xi said China is pushing forward the supply-side structural reform, boosting domestic demand, and increasing the share of the services industry in its national economy. China's economy is to maintain sound momentum of development, and China and the United States enjoy broad prospects in economic and trade cooperation, said Xi, urging the two sides to grasp the opportunity.

"China welcomes the U.S. side to participate in cooperation within the framework of the Belt and Road Initiative," said Xi.

On military relations, which he said make up an important part of bilateral ties, Xi pointed out that mutual trust in military and security areas forms the basis of the strategic mutual trust between the two countries.

Xi proposed that the two sides maintain military exchanges at various levels, give full play to such mechanisms as China-U.S. defense ministry consultations and Asia-Pacific security dialogue, and make good use of the dialogue mechanism to be established between the two countries' joint staffs of the armed forces.

Meanwhile, he suggested that the two sides carry out the annual exchange programs they have agreed upon, and implement and improve the mutual reporting mechanism on major military operations, and the code of safe conduct on naval and air military encounters. Xi also underlined the importance of further enhancing law enforcement cooperation and people-to-people exchanges.

"I think we have made tremendous progress in our relationship with China," the White House cited Trump as saying after meeting with Xi, adding that the relationship developed by Xi and himself is "outstanding." U.S. representatives have been meeting one-on-one with their Chinese counterparts, and progress has been made, said the U.S. president.

Trump said the United States is willing to further strengthen cooperation with China in economy, military affairs and people-to-people exchanges, and support China's efforts in hunting for fugitives, who have fled abroad, and recovering illicit money.

Ahead of the two presidents' second round of talks, senior Chinese and U.S. officials, on 7 April 2017, initiated the comprehensive economic dialogue and the diplomatic and security dialogue, two of the four pillars of the newly established bilateral dialogue mechanisms. Xi made the two-day trip to the southeastern U.S. coastal town of Palm Beach for the first meeting with Trump, in a bid to chart the course of bilateral ties in a new era.

While meeting with Trump in the latter's Florida resort of Mar-a-Lago, Xi said "There are a thousand reasons to make the China-U.S. relationship work, and no reason to break it."

Since the normalization of China-U.S. relations 45 years ago, the bilateral relationship, even though experienced ups and downs, has made historic progress and brought enormous and pragmatic benefits to the two peoples, Xi said.

The Chinese president said it takes political resolve and historical commitments from leaders of both countries to enhance the bilateral relations in the 45 years to come, Xinhua News Agency reported.

Xi also invited Trump to pay a state visit to China in 2017.

For his part, Trump accepted the invitation with pleasure, and hoped to make the trip at an early date, according to officials.

A Chinese commentator writes: "I should also mention the Syrian strikes. For many analysts, the timing was designed to send a message to China over North Korea. And, let us not ignore another aspect, relating to the worsening of relations between the U.S. and Russia. By default, it has increased the importance of China for both

Washington and Moscow. With all the symbolism attached to the strikes, Americans may not be in a position to simultaneously fracture ties with Russia and China. That could be one of the reasons that North Korea was not mentioned publically during the summit, although the two leaders must surely have discussed it."

7 April 2017. Bolivia requested a United Nations Security Council meeting to discuss the American strikes in Syria. Bolivia's ambassador, Sacha Sergio Llorentty Solíz, said the American strikes violated international law, and he accused the United States of acting as "attorney, judge and executioner."

8 April 2017. Sweden's foreign minister said the US attack against Syria "raises questions about how this could be compatible with international law."

11 April 2017. The UK agreed with China that there should be a political and peaceful solution to the North Korea problem.

11 April 2017. The Kremlin. Vladimir Putin met with President of Italy, Sergio Mattarella (75.7), who has come to Russia on an official visit, to discuss key aspects of Russian-Italian relations, and current international issues.

Italy's opposition parties condemned the strikes in Syria, saying, "Unilateral action is dangerous, destructive, and violates the principles of International law."

11 April 2017: from a Chinese article: A few hours after Chinese President Xi Jinping left Florida, the U.S. Carl Vinson Strike Group departed from Singapore, and sailed northward into the Western Pacific Ocean near the Korean Peninsula.
This outlines President Donald Trump's decision to employ a muscular foreign policy approach. The deployment followed his order for airstrikes against a military base in Syria. Trump had shown himself unpredictable in his first eleven weeks in office. Before his meeting with Xi, Trump had attempted to set the tone with a harsh rhetoric against the Chinese administration. "If China is not going to solve North Korea, we will," he said. Several

American think tanks have already started to elaborate on the need of American action against North Korea, examining several options after the so-called "strategic patience" expired. As China and the U.S. disagree on how to proceed with the Pyongyang imbroglio, American unilateral action would be highly risky. China prefers a wait-and-see stance on how any balance in the new multilateral world will emerge under Trump. The relationship between the U.S. and Russia is not as harmonious as numerous analysts had predicted after last November's election. The new Syrian crisis is being closely monitored by Chinese policymakers, with regard not only to the human dimension and repercussions for regional security, but also to its impact on the hypothetical rapprochement between Moscow and Washington. An interesting point is that Trump made no reference to human rights in China.

12 April 2017. Xinhua. "Chinese President Xi Jinping on Wednesday, 12 April 2017, held a telephone conversation with his U.S. counterpart, Donald Trump, and discussed the situation on the Korean Peninsula and in Syria. Xi said that China sticks to the target of the denuclearization of the Korean Peninsula, and that China is committed to peace and stability of the peninsula.
China holds that the issue should be solved through peaceful means, said Xi, adding that his country is ready to maintain communication and coordination with the United States on the issue.
On Syria, Xi said that any use of chemical weapons is unacceptable, and that the path of political settlement should be followed.
He expressed the hope that the UN Security Council would speak in one voice, as it is important for the Security Council to remain united over the issue. Xi also asked teams of China and the United States to work together closely to make sure that Trump's visit to China later this year could achieve fruitful results.
He also urged the two sides to promote economic cooperation, expand exchanges in military, law enforcement, cyber and people-to-people areas, enhance communication and coordination in major global and regional issues, through the newly established four-pronged dialogue mechanism. He expressed the hope that the dialogue mechanism will yield as many early-stage results as possible, so as to inject impetus to bilateral relations.

The four-pronged dialogue mechanism, which covers the fields of foreign affairs and security, economy, law enforcement and cybersecurity, social and people-to-people exchanges, is an important result of Xi's meeting with Trump in Florida.

Xi said his recent tete-a-tete with Trump, in the latter's Mar-a-Lago estate in Florida, has produced important results, which have won positive response among the Chinese people and the international community. The two leaders held in-depth discussions and reached important consensus on bilateral relations in the new era, and on major global and regional issues, said Xi.

He and Trump have increased mutual understanding, and established sound working relations, he added.

In Wednesday's phone conversation, Trump said the meeting with Xi at Mar-a-Lago was a success. It is very important for the two presidents to maintain close communication, he added.

Trump agreed that the two sides should work together to promote pragmatic cooperation in wide-ranging areas.

He said he was looking forward to his state visit to China this year. The two presidents agreed to keep close communication through all kinds of channels."

After this article, The White House released this comment: "President Donald J. Trump spoke last night with President Xi Jinping of China, to follow up after President Xi's visit to Mar-a-Lago. It was a very productive call."

China's Foreign Ministry, when addressing questions on the US strikes on Syria, said the country opposes the use of force in international affairs, but also reiterated its stance opposing the use of chemical weapons. "China always opposes the use of force in international affairs and we advocate resolving disputes peacefully through dialogues. ... We always hold that the Syrian issue should be resolved through political means."

12 April 2017. Xinhua: "Any attempt to play up the case of a Taiwan resident under investigation will further harm the "already severe" relations between the mainland and Taiwan, an official said Wednesday, 12 April 2017. Lee Ming-che is being investigated for suspected activities "endangering national security," An Fengshan,

spokesperson for the Taiwan Affairs Office of the State Council, said at a press conference.

12 April 2017. From a Chinese article "Reminder: North Korea is not Syria": "As the USS Carl Vinson Carrier strike group steams north towards the Korean peninsula, the question that confronts us all is: will North Korea be next?
Over six years of civil war has left Syria in no position to defend against any external force, much less some random missile strikes by the United States. It cannot defend itself against any army or mercenaries from pretty much all the countries around it. It cannot defend itself against airstrikes by Israel. It is a rump of a state that once existed, and, truth be told, probably will never be whole again, or unified under a common single ruler, much like Afghanistan or Libya. North Korea is different."

13 April 2017. The Kremlin. Vladimir Putin met with First Vice Premier of the State Council of China, Zhang Gaoli (71).

13 April 2017. Vladimir Putin had a telephone conversation with President of Turkey Recep Tayyip Erdogan (63) at the initiative of the Turkish side.
The discussion covered the situation in Syria. The presidents expressed their mutual commitment to further joint efforts to consolidate the ceasefire regime and foster the intra-Syrian negotiating process in both the Astana and Geneva formats.
The two leaders spoke in favor of an objective and thorough international investigation to be conducted as soon as possible into the use of chemical weapons in the town of Khan Sheihoun on April 4, 2017.
While addressing bilateral issues, the heads of state agreed to direct their governments to intensify their efforts to implement the decisions of the sixth meeting of the High Level Cooperation Council that took place in Moscow on March 10, 2017.
They agreed to maintain their contact.
Turkish President Erdogan narrowly won a crucial referendum on 16 April 2017, which will greatly expand the powers of his office, and cement his hold on power. Voters approved a set of constitutional amendments that give Erdogan greater sway over

policy, including the authority to appoint ministers, and top judges at his discretion.

14 April 2017. Xinhua. China urges restraint amid Korean Peninsula tensions. Beijing urged Washington, Seoul and Pyongyang on Friday, 14 April, to stop irritating and threatening each other, to prevent the situation on the Korean Peninsula from sliding to the point of being irreparable.

"There has been heightened tension between the United States, the Republic of Korea and the Democratic People's Republic of Korea. The precarious situation deserves our attention and concern," Foreign Minister Wang Yi said during a joint news conference with his visiting French counterpart, Jean-Marc Ayrault.

"We urge all parties to refrain from inflammatory or threatening statements and deeds, to prevent the situation on the Korean Peninsula from becoming irreversible."

"Once a war really happens, the result will be nothing but loss all around. No one can become a winner," Wang said.

He added that "no matter who it is, if it wants to make war or trouble on the Korean Peninsula, it must take the historical responsibility, and pay the due price".

17 April 2017. Xinhua: The Shanghai Cooperation Organization (SCO) is a political, economic and security forum bringing together China, Russia and the Central Asian states of Tajikistan, Kazakhstan, Kyrgyzstan and Uzbekistan. In a matter of weeks, Pakistan and India will complete the requirements to attain full membership at the upcoming summit in June.

17 April 2017. Xinhua: North Korea is the latest flash-point of conflict on the global scene; tensions are simmering since the U.S. installed its highly advanced "hit to kill" 100% efficient THAAD missile defense system in South Korea to counter N. Korea's missile capability. Lately, President Trump has also been tweeting the U.S. could solve the North Korea "problem" without China if needed. His recent remarks on the issue have been quite direct and definite. "I don't talk about the military," he said. "We are sending an Armada, very powerful. We have submarines, very powerful. Far more powerful than the aircraft carrier, that I can tell you. And we have

the best military people. And I will say this: He is doing the wrong thing." The USS Carl Vinson's presence in the Korean peninsula could be a warning to keep Pyongyang at bay but the situation is unpredictable.

18 April 2017. Newspapers write that China and Russia have dispatched spy vessels to shadow a US aircraft carrier group heading to North Korean waters.

18 April 2017. "Canada does not accept the contention that Canada's dairy policies are the cause of financial loss for dairy farmers in the U.S.," Canadian Ambassador David MacNaughton said in rebuttal to President Trump's surprise criticism on Tuesday, 18 April 2017. Trump leveled the trade threats during an event in Wisconsin, where he unveiled his "Buy American-Hire American" executive order.

18 April 2017. From a Chinese article: A photo shows a submarine-launched ballistic missile, which was displayed during a military parade in central Pyongyang, on 15 April 2017. Among the possible, but the least desirable, responses to the Democratic People's Republic of Korea's nuclear and missile tests (although its last one on Sunday, 16 April 2017, was a failure) could be a preemptive strike by the United States. There is no guarantee, though, that the presumed US strike would be precise enough to wipe out all nuclear facilities in the DPRK, before Pyongyang launches a nuclear attack in retaliation.

If that happens, the DPRK won't wait to fire its nuclear missiles, and thousands of howitzers and rocket launchers, deployed along the 38th parallel Military Demarcation Line, into the Republic of Korea. No defense systems, including the US Terminal High Altitude Area Defense anti-missile system, will be able to shield off such a shower of artillery shells. And Pyongyang's missiles could destroy Seoul and hit even Japan.

Talks are the only way to resolve the issue. But how can the US be persuaded to hold talks with the DPRK? Having fired 59 Tomahawk missiles on Syria on April 6, 2017, the Donald Trump administration seems anxious to use force to showcase its political resolve. The US doesn't want to be seen as being blackmailed by a country it has labeled a "rogue state". That is why Washington has rejected all proposals by Pyongyang for bilateral talks. Besides, it believes that the Six-Party Talks were useful only in giving the DPRK the needed time to develop nuclear weapons.

18 April 2017: From a Chinese article: Donald Trump and Xi Jinping met in Mar-a-Lago, and since that time the world has once again turned upside down. The most notable changes, since the meeting, are Trump's international reversals on China, Russia, Syria, Afghanistan and NATO; and domestic reversals on Fed Chair, low interest rates, the Export-Import Bank, advisor Steve Bannon and FBI Director James Comey.

Chinese navy commissions submarine killer stealth warship for service in South China Sea.

19 April 2017. Xinhua: Chinese President Xi Jinping, who is also general secretary of the Communist Party of China Central Committee, and chairman of the Central Military Commission, asked People's Liberation Army commanders on Tuesday, 18 April 2017, to focus on strengthening their unit's combat capability, following the establishment of 84 large units. Xi met commanders of these new units at the commission's headquarters in Beijing.
The new units must prepare themselves for combat and study wars. They should concentrate on improving their joint operation capabilities and technology level, Xi said.
The president also told the new forces to conduct more combat exercises and give priority to building "new-type" fighting capabilities.

19 April 2017. Senior officials of China and the European Union (EU) agreed Wednesday 19 April 2017, to enhance coordination on global issues, continue to promote improvement to global governance and work together for more inclusive, balanced, sustainable globalization.

From the WSJ: Chinese state-backed hackers have recently targeted South Korean entities involved in deploying a U.S. missile-defense system, says an American cybersecurity firm, despite Beijing's denial of retaliation against Seoul over the issue.

In recent weeks, two cyberespionage groups that the firm linked to Beijing's military and intelligence agencies have launched a variety of attacks against South Korea's government, military, defense companies and a big conglomerate, John Hultquist, director of cyberespionage analysis at FireEye Inc., said in an interview.

The California-based firm, which counts South Korean agencies as clients, including one that oversees internet security, wouldn't name the targets.

20 April 2017. President Trump on Thursday 20 April 2017, launched a trade probe against China and other exporters of cheap steel into the U.S. market, raising the possibility of new tariffs. He also turned his focus to America's northern neighbor. "We're not going to let Canada take advantage," Trump declared, vowing to get to the "negotiating table" swiftly.

20 April 2017. Indonesian President Widodo (55) said that, as the largest Muslim population country in the world, as well as the third largest democracy in the world (after India and the USA), Indonesia also agrees to strengthen cooperation with the U. S. on peace.

21 April 2017. From an official Chinese article: Chinese President Xi Jinping, who is also general secretary of the Communist Party of China (CPC) Central Committee, and chairman of the Central Military Commission (CMC), spoke at a meeting during an inspection of the Southern Theater Command of the People's Liberation Army (PLA), on 21 April 2017.

Chinese President Xi Jinping inspected the Southern Theater Command of the People's Liberation Army (PLA) on Friday 21 April 2017, and stressed building a strong army.

Xi urged all military personnel to resolutely safeguard the authority of CPC Central Committee, and unswervingly follow the Party's leadership. He asked all military personnel to greet the 19th CPC National Congress, scheduled for later this year, with outstanding achievements. Noting that 2017 is of great significance for the Party and the country, Xi urged the PLA to strengthen ideological building, combat preparation and reform implementation.

22 April 2017. From news reports: China has protested a visit by Philippine military chiefs to a disputed island in the South China Sea, but Manila maintained on Saturday 22 April 2017, it owns the territory where Filipino troops and villagers have lived for decades. After Philippine President Rodrigo Duterte took office in June 2016, he moved to renew Manila's friendship with Beijing, which has been strained by territorial disputes.

Philippine Defense Secretary Delfin Lorenzana and military chief of staff General Eduardo Ano flew to the island, which Filipinos call Pag-asa (which is internationally known as Thitu, and is called Zhongye Dao by China; it's the second-largest island in the South China Sea's hotly contested Spratlys archipelago), with dozens of journalists, on Friday 21 April 2017, to inspect an eroded airstrip.

In Beijing, foreign ministry spokesman Lu Kang expressed China's displeasure over the high-profile Philippine visits to the island, saying Beijing was "gravely concerned about and dissatisfied" by the island visits, adding it "has lodged representations with the Philippine side". "We hope that the Philippine side could cherish the hard-won sound momentum of development the bilateral relations are experiencing, faithfully follow the consensus reached between the two leaderships, maintain general peace and stability in the South China Sea," Lu said. The Philippine government replied by saying the island was part of an island municipality under its western province of Palawan, which faces the disputed waters.

"Our visits there are part of the government mandate to ensure the safety, wellbeing, livelihood and personal security of our citizens there," Department of Foreign Affairs spokesman Robespierre Bolivar said in a statement. During the trip to Pag-asa, Chinese forces tried to drive away two Philippine air force planes that carried Lorenzana, Ano and others as they flew near a Chinese man-made island called Subi, just 25 km away.

Lorenzana said their aircraft continued uninterrupted without any incident, after Filipino pilots messaged back to the Chinese that they were flying over Philippine territory. The Chinese warned the Philippine aircraft they were entering the periphery of Chinese installations, and told to avoid miscalculation.

The Chinese navy has similarly warned US ships and aircraft to leave what Beijing claims as its territory, messages the Americans also ignored.

China claims virtually the entire sea and has aggressively tried to fortify its foothold by transforming, in recent years, seven mostly submerged reefs into island outposts, including Subi.

Three of the artificial islands were built with runways, along with buildings, towers, radars and more recently weapons systems, to the consternation of other Asian claimant governments, and the United States, which insists on freedom of navigation in international waters.

24 April 2017, Xinhua: Chinese President Xi Jinping (who is also general secretary of the Communist Party of China (CPC) Central Committee, and chairman of the Central Military Commission (CMC)) and his U.S. counterpart Donald Trump, on Monday 24 April 2017, discussed bilateral ties and the situation on the Korean Peninsula on phone, pledging close contact, by various means, to promptly exchange views on major issues of common concern. China strongly opposes any act that violates resolutions of the United Nations Security Council, Xi said, and hopes that the parties concerned will exercise restraint, and refrain from taking any action that will aggravate tensions on the Peninsula.

Xi noted that only when the parties concerned shoulder their due responsibilities, and meet each other halfway, can they solve the nuclear issue of the Democratic People's Republic of Korea, and denuclearize the Korean Peninsula as soon as possible.

He said China is willing to work, and make every effort, with all parties concerned, including the United States, to realize peace on the Korean Peninsula, and in Northeast Asia, and the world at large. The Chinese president recalled that he reached important consensus with Trump during a meeting at the latter's Mar-a-Lago estate in Florida earlier this month, and that they had very good communication recently, which has won positive evaluation by the Chinese and American peoples, and the rest of the international community. With a rapid change of the international situation, it is quite necessary for China and the United States to keep close contact, and to exchange views on important issues, in a timely manner, said Xi. He stressed that China and the United States should implement the consensus reached between them, and consolidate the momentum of steady development of bilateral relations.

Xi also urged the working teams of China and the United States to strengthen coordination on a good preparation for Trump's visit to China later this year, and for the early opening of a four-pronged bilateral dialogue mechanism.

The establishment of the four-pronged dialogue mechanism, which covers the fields of foreign affairs and security, economy, law enforcement and cybersecurity, social and people-to-people exchanges, is an important result of Xi's meeting with Trump in Florida. He also urged the two sides to promote economic and trade cooperation, expand exchanges in military, law enforcement, cyber and people-to-people areas, enhance communication on major global and regional issues, and promote China-U.S. relations toward continued achievement of new development.

In the phone call, Trump said he had a very good meeting with President Xi at Mar-a-Lago, noting that he is also satisfied with the development of the two countries' relations, and that he is respectful to the Chinese people.

Trump said that it is very important for the United States and China to keep close contact, and maintain coordination on major issues.

The U.S. president expected to meet Xi again at an early date, and looked forward to paying a state visit to China.

24 April 2017. On the same phone conversation described above by an official Chinese article, the White House writes: President Donald J. Trump spoke yesterday (Sunday 23 April 2017 evening in Washington, USA, is Monday 24 April 2017 morning in Beijing, China) with President Xi Jinping of China, to address issues regarding North Korea. President Trump criticized North Korea's continued belligerence, and emphasized that Pyongyang's actions are destabilizing the Korean Peninsula. The two leaders reaffirmed the urgency of the threat posed by North Korea's missile and nuclear programs, and committed to strengthen coordination in achieving the denuclearization of the Korean Peninsula.

China created the Asian Infrastructure Investment Bank in 2015, in a development, many caution, will increase its global leadership position to an uncomfortable level.

Democracy promotion organizations such as the China Alliance for Democracy, the Federation for a Democratic China and the Independent Federation of Chinese Students and Scholars emphasized that, while 79% of the American people opposed China's entry into the World Trade Organization, some U. S. politicians ignored this.

25 April 2017. For the third time in two months, **a** federal judge has stopped an immigration order by President Trump, which sought to withhold funding from "sanctuary cities" that don't cooperate with immigration officials.

A Statement from the White House on Sanctuary Cities Ruling starts with: "Today, the rule of law suffered another blow, as an unelected judge unilaterally rewrote immigration policy for our Nation."

26 April 2017. The White House. Late this afternoon, President Donald J. Trump spoke with both President Peña Nieto of Mexico and Prime Minister Trudeau of Canada. Both conversations were pleasant and productive. President Trump agreed not to terminate NAFTA at this time, and the leaders agreed to proceed swiftly, according to their required internal procedures, to enable the renegotiation of the NAFTA deal, to the benefit of all three countries. President Trump said, "it is my privilege to bring NAFTA up to date through renegotiation. It is an honor to deal with both President Peña Nieto and Prime Minister Trudeau, and I believe that the end result will make all three countries stronger and better."

26 April 2017. In the middle of high tensions on the Korean Peninsula, the U.S. military has started moving key parts of its THAAD anti-missile defense system, to a deployment site in South Korea. The move, which has angered North Korea, China and Russia, prompted protests by hundreds of local residents, and was denounced by the frontrunner in South Korea's presidential election.

26 April 2017. Canadian Prime Minister Justin Trudeau told President Trump in a phone call that he "refuted the baseless allegations" that persuaded Washington to introduce a 20% tariff on

softwood lumber from Canada. "Canada has made business for our dairy farmers in Wisconsin, and other border states, very difficult. We will not stand for this. Watch!" Trump wrote in a tweet.

27 April 2017. The White House. Joint Statement from President Donald J. Trump and President Mauricio Macri (59).
President Donald J. Trump hosted President Mauricio Macri of Argentina today to discuss ways to deepen the close partnership between the United States and Argentina.

27 April 2017. Russian President Vladimir Putin held a meeting in Moscow with Prime Minister of Japan Shinzo Abe. The agenda included implementation of the agreements reached during Mr. Putin's visit to Japan on December 15–16, 2016, and the prospects for developing bilateral cooperation in the political, trade, economic and humanitarian spheres.

27 April 2017. Faced with growing criticism from the bloc over its handling of a major crisis, Venezuela is quitting the Organization of American States. Foreign Minister Delcy Rodriguez branded the hemisphere's oldest regional alliance an "interventionist coalition" led by Washington. The announcement late Wednesday, 26 April, will raise international tension over Venezuela, where unrest has left 28 people dead this month.

29 April 2017. From Reuters. North Korea test-fired a ballistic missile on Saturday 29 April 2017, shortly after U.S. Secretary of State Rex Tillerson warned that, failure to curb Pyongyang's nuclear and ballistic missile programs, could lead to "catastrophic consequences". U.S. and South Korean officials said the test, from an area north of the North Korean capital, appeared to have failed, in what would be the North's fourth straight unsuccessful missile test since March 2017.

29 April 2017. "North Korea disrespected the wishes of China & its highly respected President, when it launched, though unsuccessfully, a missile today. Bad!" President Trump tweeted on Saturday 29 April 2017.

In a new article in the National Communication Association's Review of Communication, researchers explore the connection between gratitude expression, and psychological and physical well-being. Expressing gratitude makes us healthier.

Robots are helping children with autism, regarding their social skills in schools and hospitals.

Artificial Intelligence and robot integration is essential in major industries, including healthcare, education, manufacturing, energy and transportation.

"Peace is not an absence of war, it is a virtue, a state of mind, a disposition for benevolence, confidence, justice." – Benedictus Spinoza – Dutch philosopher (1632 – 1677 (age 44)).

Washington, DC: Woodrow Wilson International Center for Scholars (founded 1968). In 2013 there was the 1913 Centennial, in celebration of the 100th anniversary of President (1913-1921) Woodrow Wilson's (1856-1924) inauguration.

Chapter 5. May 2017

2 May 2017. "Our country needs a good 'shutdown' in September to fix mess!" President Trump tweeted on Tuesday, 2 May 2017, calling for voters to elect more Republican Senators in 2018, or to undercut the ability to block legislation with filibusters. The suggestion is to "change the rules now to 51%", which was deployed by the GOP during the Gorsuch Supreme Court voting.

2 May 2017. The White House. Washington, D.C. President Donald J. Trump of the United States, and President Vladimir Putin of the Russian Federation spoke today (2 May 2017) regarding Syria. President Trump and President Putin agreed that the suffering in Syria has gone on for far too long, and that all parties must do all they can to end the violence. The conversation was a very good one, and included the discussion of safe, or de-escalation, zones to achieve lasting peace for humanitarian, and many other reasons. The United States will be sending a representative to the cease-fire talks in Astana, Kazakhstan, on May 3-4, 2017. They also discussed at length working together to eradicate terrorism throughout the Middle East. Finally, they spoke about how best to resolve the very dangerous situation in North Korea.

2 May 2017. The same telephone conversation described above, but now from Russia: Vladimir Putin had a telephone conversation with President of the United States, Donald Trump. A wide range of current issues regarding the two countries' cooperation in the international arena was discussed, with an emphasis on future coordination of Russian and US actions to fight international terrorism, in the context of the Syrian crisis.

It was agreed to bolster the dialogue between the heads of the two nations' foreign policy agencies, in an effort to find ways to stabilize the ceasefire, and make it durable and manageable.

The aim is to create preconditions for launching a real settlement process in Syria. To that end, the Russian Foreign Minister and the US Secretary of State shall promptly brief the countries' leaders on any progress achieved.

The dangerous situation on the Korean Peninsula was thoroughly discussed. The President of Russia called for restraint, and an easing of tensions. It was agreed to organize joint work aimed at achieving diplomatic solutions, and a comprehensive settlement of the problem.

Vladimir Putin and Donald Trump agreed to continue their telephone contacts, and spoke in favor of arranging a personal meeting during the G20 Summit in Hamburg, on July 7–8.

The conversation was businesslike and constructive.

2 May 2017. Germany's Chancellor met with Russian President in Sochi, Russia.

3 May 2017. Republican Senator Rand Paul, MD, on Omnibus Spending Bill: "Looking at all the smiling faces on the other side of the aisle, I have to ask: are Democrats still the minority party? You would be tempted to think the $1 trillion government funding deal is like Christmas morning for them, as Republicans have handed them free media to brag about how much of the President's agenda they have stopped. You'll see it in the news as an "Omnibus spending bill," when it should really be called "the Status Quo Protection Act." "

Economists have found that the most widely used model, for predicting how U.S. government spending affects gross domestic product (GDP), can be rigged using theoretical assumptions to control forecasts.

3 May 2017. From an official Chinese article. Chinese President Xi Jinping and his Philippine counterpart, Rodrigo Duterte, held a telephone conversation Wednesday, 3 May, discussing bilateral ties and regional cooperation. Xi said he met Duterte twice last year, and reached important agreements with him. As a result, bilateral ties greatly improved, said Xi.

4 May 2017. Russia, Iran and Turkey are setting up four safe zones in Syria, which the United Nations described as a promising step to wind down the brutal six-year war. Quoting Russian envoy at Syria peace talks, Alexander Lavrentyev, Russian news agencies

reported that U.S. and coalition warplanes will not be allowed to fly over the "de-escalation areas."

4 May 2017. "China should no longer recklessly try to test the limitations of our patience," said the commentary released by North Korea's official news agency KCNA, warning it could trigger "grave consequences." KCNA added that China has regularly "infringed upon the strategic interests" in becoming closer to the U.S., and thus committed a "betrayal" in the process.

Many observers say that Communist North Korea wants to imitate Communist North Vietnam, which, after 20 years of war against America and South Vietnam (1955-1975), succeeded to occupy South Vietnam, and now, for over 42 years, there is only one Communist Vietnam.

5 May 2017. President Donald J. Trump met with Prime Minister Malcolm Turnbull of Australia on May 4, 2017, in New York City. The President thanked Prime Minister Turnbull (62) for traveling to New York for the commemoration of the 75th anniversary of the Battle of the Coral Sea, a gesture which shows the deep ties between the United States and Australia.

6 May 2017. National Security Advisor McMaster met with Venezuela's National Assembly President Julio Borges (47) at the White House yesterday afternoon. They discussed the ongoing crisis in Venezuela and the need for the government to adhere to the Venezuelan Constitution, release political prisoners, respect the National Assembly, and hold free and democratic elections. They agreed that there is a strong need to bring the crisis to a quick and peaceful conclusion.

7 May 2017. Emmanuel Macron (born 21 Dec 1977, age 39, studied philosophy) is set to become the youngest president in French history, after winning 66% of Sunday's (7 May) runoff vote.

7 May 2017. North Korea detained the U.S. citizen and Professor Kim Hak Song over the weekend, raising to four the

number of Americans being held by the nation's authoritarian regime.

North Korea's ambassador to the U.K. said the country is preparing for its sixth nuclear test.

8 May 2017. President Donald J. Trump spoke today with President-elect Emmanuel Macron of France, to congratulate him on his victory in the May 7th French presidential election. President Trump emphasized his desire to work closely with President-elect Macron in confronting shared challenges, and noted the long and robust history of cooperation between the United States and its oldest ally, France. The two leaders agreed to spend time together during the May 25th NATO leaders meeting in Brussels.

8 May 2017. President Donald J. Trump spoke today with President Pedro Pablo Kuczynski of Peru, to address the deteriorating political and economic crisis in Venezuela. President Trump underscored that the United States will work together with Peru in seeking to improve democratic institutions, and help the people of Venezuela. President Kuczynski expressed his gratitude for President Trump's prompt humanitarian assistance in response to the devastating floods in Peru.

9 May 2017. From the White House: We congratulate President-elect Moon Jae-in and join the people of the Republic of Korea in celebrating their peaceful, democratic transition of power. We look forward to working with President-elect Moon to continue to strengthen the alliance between the United States and the Republic of Korea, and to deepen the enduring friendship and partnership between our two countries.

9 May 2017. From an official Chinese article: In their first telephone talk, President Xi Jinping and French president-elect Emmanuel Macron agreed on Tuesday, 9 May, to maintain contact and meet each other at an early date. The phone conversation, reaffirming a shared commitment to tackle a range of global issues, came a day after Xi sent a congratulatory message on Monday, 8 May, to Macron, on his victory the day before.

9 May 2017. President Trump has approved plans to directly arm Kurdish fighters battling ISIS, as they close in on their capital of Raqqa. Turkey, a NATO ally, considers the Kurdish organization YPG to be a terrorist group that threatens its borders. The move also comes ahead of President Erdogan's first meeting, next week, with Trump in Washington.

9 May 2017. The White House: Today, President Donald J. Trump informed FBI Director James Comey (56) that he has been terminated, and removed from office. President Trump acted based on the clear recommendations of both Deputy Attorney General Rod Rosenstein, and Attorney General Jeff Sessions (70).

The U. S. Bureau of Labor Statistics says that there are 5.7 millions of job openings, and 7.1 millions of unemployed in the U. S.

10 May 2017. Moon Jae-in (64) has been sworn in as president of South Korea. He took 41.1% of the vote, promising to expand the nation's economy, improve relations with the North, and seek more balanced diplomacy towards the U.S. and China.

On Wednesday, 10 May, night, South Korea President Moon held his first phone conversation with U.S. President Donald Trump, and talked about the Peninsula situations. Trump officially invited Moon to the United States.

11 May 2017. Mexico has sent an unambiguous message to the U.S., saying an upcoming visit by government officials to China showed the country had other places to export to, if NAFTA gets torn up. "We will use (the China visit) geopolitically, as strategic leverage," declared Mexican Economy Minister Ildefonso Guajardo. "It sends the signal that we have many alternatives."

11 May 2017. From official Chinese Xinhua: Chinese President Xi Jinping holds a welcome ceremony for Vietnamese President Tran Dai Quang (60), before their talks in Beijing, capital of China, May 11, 2017.

Chinese President Xi Jinping held talks Thursday 11 May, with Vietnamese President Tran Dai Quang, and both agreed to boost bilateral all-round strategic cooperative partnership up to a new stage. Xi recalled his meeting with Quang last November on the sidelines of the Asia-Pacific Economic Cooperation (APEC) Economic Leaders' Meeting in Lima of Peru, in which they reached important consensus on deepening bilateral all-round strategic cooperation. Xi invited Nguyen Phu Trong, general secretary of the Communist Party of Vietnam (CPV) Central Committee, to visit China in January this year. Xi and Trong had in-depth exchanges on major issues of common concern, and clarified the direction of future China-Vietnam ties. Xi said both sides should work closely to implement consensus reached by state leaders, cement cooperation in various areas, and boost their all-round strategic partnership to a new level. "The two countries should boost maritime cooperation, accumulate consensus, and expand common interests, and control their differences through dialogue," Xi said.

11 May 2017. From Xinhua official Chinese article: Chinese President Xi Jinping held a phone conversation with newly-elected South Korean President Moon Jae-in on Thursday, 11 May.
Congratulating Moon on his election as South Korean president, Xi said that China and South Korea are close neighbors, as well as important players in the region. Since the two countries established diplomatic relations 25 years ago, their ties have achieved enormous achievements that deserve to be cherished, Xi said.
Both sides should respect each other's major concerns and legitimate interests, and try best to seek common ground, and handle disputes properly, Xi said.

12 May 2017, from official Chinese Xinhua: President Xi Jinping and his wife, Peng Liyuan, and Uzbekistan's President Shavkat Mirziyoyev (59) and his wife, Ziroatkhon Hoshimova, attended a welcoming ceremony outside the Great Hall of the People in Beijing, on May 12, 2017.
Chinese and Uzbekistani enterprises signed agreements and deals of more than $10 billion, just days before the Belt and Road Forum for International Cooperation. The deals were signed during Uzbekistani President Shavkat Mirziyoyev's first state visit to

China, which began on Thursday, 11 May, Assistant Foreign Minister Li Huilai said on Friday, 12 May. Mirziyoyev will also attend the forum in Beijing on Sunday and Monday, 14 and 15 May.

In his meeting with Mirziyoyev on Friday, President Xi Jinping said Uzbekistan is a close and important neighbor of China. Xi said Uzbekistan was among the first countries to support and participate in the building of the Belt and Road Initiative.

12 May 2017, from Chinese official Xinhua: Chinese President Xi Jinping meets with Polish Prime Minister Beata Szydlo (54) at the Great Hall of the People in Beijing, capital of China, May 12, 2017. Beata Szydlo is in Beijing to attend the Belt and Road Forum for International Cooperation.

12 May 2017. From official Chinese Xinhua: Chinese President Xi Jinping said Friday 12 May 2017, that Mongolia is welcome to actively participate in construction of the Belt and Road. China supports Mongolia's efforts to be a bridge linking European and Asian continents, Xi told Mongolian Prime Minister Jargaltulga Erdenebat (43), who is in Beijing to attend the Belt and Road Forum for International Cooperation scheduled for May 14 to 15.

12 May 2017. From Xinhua: "South Korean President Moon Jae-in will send special envoys to China to discuss issues concerning the U.S. Terminal High Altitude Area Defense (THAAD), and the Democratic People's Republic of Korea (DPRK), a senior presidential press secretary said on Thursday, 11 May. Yoon Young-chan told a press conference in Seoul on Thursday that President Moon would dispatch separate delegations to discuss THAAD and the DPRK's nuclear program with their Chinese counterparts, although the two issues will be dealt with together.
Yoon said the dispatches were mentioned during the first telephone conversation between Moon and Chinese President Xi Jinping which lasted for 40 minutes beginning at about noon, on 11 May.

13 May 2017. From the White House. "The President has been briefed on the latest missile test by North Korea (on 14 May morning in North Korea, but on 13 May evening in Washington, DC, USA).

14 May 2017, in China: Vladimir Putin (64.5) held talks with President of China Xi Jinping (63.8). The talks covered, in particular, the prospects of economic cooperation between Russia and China, and topical international issues. The Russian President congratulated his Chinese counterpart on the successful opening of the One Belt, One Road international forum, and pointed out that the event is well-timed. Vladimir Putin and Xi Jinping also discussed the Chinese President's upcoming visit to Russia.

14 May 2017. Paris, France. Emmanuel Macron (age 39.4) was sworn in as French president on Sunday, 14 May, promising to return confidence to a nation that had been "broken" by a spate of terrorist attacks, and a sluggish economy.

14 May 2017, Beijing, China. Newspapers announced that the Belt and Road Forum opened in Beijing on May 14. The two-day forum is dedicated to President Xi Jinping's foreign policy project, the Belt and Road Initiative (also known as "One Belt, One Road" after its two main components: the Silk Road Economic Belt, and the 21st Century Maritime Silk Road). China has advertised the forum as the major international event of the year, with 29 heads of state or government (Russia, Mongolia, Kazakhstan, Vietnam, Cambodia, Laos, Fiji, Indonesia, Philippines, Malaysia, Pakistan, Uzbekistan, Kyrgyzstan, Turkey, Greece, Czech Republic, Serbia, Slovakia, Italy, Switzerland, Hungary, Belarus, Poland, Spain, Ethiopia, Kenya, Sri Lanka, Argentina, Chile) to be in attendance (along with, of course, Xi himself). International organizations will be well-represented too, with UN Secretary General António Guterres (68), President of the World Bank Jim Yong Kim (57), and Managing Director of the International Monetary Fund Christine Lagarde (61) all set to attend. Chinese media has also highlighted the level of global interest by citing the number of countries to be represented: up to 130 (including USA, UK, France, Japan, Germany, Australia, New Zeeland, Brazil, Romania, Finland, Singapore, South Korea, Egypt, Iran, Saudi Arabia, Thailand, Azerbaijan, Nepal, Tunisia, Kuwait, UAE, Ukraine, Bangladesh, Afghanistan, Syria, North Korea, Maldives, Myanmar).

President Xi hailed his country's initiative as "the project of the century".

15 May 2017. From the White House. President Donald J. Trump welcomed Crown Prince Mohamed bin Zayed Al Nahyan (56) of the United Arab Emirates to the White House today, to discuss steps to deepen our strategic partnership, and promote stability and prosperity throughout the Middle East.

15 May 2017. The EU's need for deep reforms is so dire that even the idea of changing the EU treaty is "not taboo," French President Emmanuel Macron said, during his first joint news conference with Angela Merkel. "First, we need to work on what we want to change, and then, if it turns out it needs a treaty change, then we're prepared to do that," the German Chancellor declared.

15 May 2017. Following Washington's exit from the TPP, the 11 remaining members (Australia, Brunei, Canada, Chile, Japan, Malaysia, Mexico, New Zeeland, Peru, Singapore and Vietnam) have kick-started discussions on how to proceed without the U.S., and recently wrapped up talks in Toronto, Canada. "Since we have come thus far, Japan must now take on a leadership role, and bring the talks forward," Shinzo Abe told CNBC. "Momentum" should not be lost, he added, but left the door open for a U.S. return to the deal.

15 May 2017, Seoul, South Korea, from Reuters - North Korea said on Monday, 15 May, it had successfully conducted a newly developed mid-to-long range missile test on Sunday, 14 May, supervised by leader Kim Jong Un, and aimed at verifying the capability to carry a "large scale heavy nuclear warhead."
The North fired a ballistic missile that landed in the north of the Sea of Japan, near the city Olga in Russia, on Sunday, in a launch that Washington called a message to South Korea, days after its new president took office, pledging to engage Pyongyang in dialog.
The missile was launched at the highest angle so as not to affect the security of neighboring countries, and flew 787 kilometers reaching an altitude of 2,111.5 kilometers, official North Korea agency KCNA said. "The test-fire aimed at verifying the tactical and

technological specifications of the newly developed ballistic rocket, capable of carrying a large-size heavy nuclear warhead," KCNA said. North Korea is believed to be developing an intercontinental ballistic missile (ICBM), capable of carrying a nuclear warhead, and reaching the mainland United States. The U.S. military's Pacific Command said the type of missile that was fired was "not consistent with an intercontinental ballistic missile."

15 May 2017. Beijing. President Xi Jinping on Monday, !5 May, called on China and the Philippines to step up communication on major issues concerning bilateral ties, in order to lead their relations toward healthy and stable development.

15 May 2017. Beijing. President Xi Jinping said Monday, 15 May, that China is willing to work with Kenya to push forward bilateral ties.

16 May 2017. The White House. President Tayyip Erdogan said there are "outstanding" American relations, on Tuesday, 16 May, but emphasized Turkey will not accept Syrian Kurdish fighters in the region, while stopping short of directly criticizing a U.S. decision to arm them. "We've had a great relationship, and we will make it even better," President Trump said in a joint appearance, calling Erdogan a strong ally in the fight against terrorism.

16 May 2017. Beijing. Chinese President Xi Jinping on Tuesday, 16 May, suggested docking the Belt and Road Initiative with the European Investment Plan, in order to inject new momentum into China-EU ties (European Union (EU, 28 member states, population over 510 M)

16 May 2017. Beijing. Chinese President Xi Jinping, on Tuesday, 16 May, met with Toshihiro Nikai (78), secretary-general of Japan's ruling Liberal Democratic Party, expressing the hope that joint efforts will be made to ensure bilateral ties develop in the right direction.

16 May2017. Beijing. President Xi Jinping said Tuesday, 16 May, that China is willing to deepen the all-weather friendship with Serbia, to boost their comprehensive strategic partnership.

16 May 2017. Beijing. President Xi Jinping met with his Kyrgyz counterpart Almazbek Atambayev (60) in Beijing on Tuesday, 16 May, vowing to push forward the bilateral partnership.

16 May 2017. Beijing. Chinese President Xi Jinping on Tuesday, 16 May, called for deepening cooperation with Laos, and creating better future for bilateral ties, by taking the opportunity of jointly promoting the Belt and Road Initiative.

16 May 2017. Beijing. President Xi Jinping said Tuesday, 16 May, that China is willing to continue to provide Myanmar with assistance in its internal peace progress.

16 May 2017. Beijing. President Xi Jinping on Tuesday, 16 May, called for more efforts to advance the strategic partnership of cooperation between China and Sri Lanka.

16 May 2017. Beijing. Chinese President Xi Jinping said Tuesday, 16 May, that China is ready to enhance all-round cooperation with Fiji, for the benefit of the people in both countries.

16 May 2017. Seoul. "The reality is that there is a high possibility of a military conflict at the NLL (Northern Limit Line) and military demarcation line," declared South Korea's newly-elected President Moon Jae-in. He also said Pyongyang's nuclear and missile capabilities seem to have advanced rapidly recently, but Seoul was ready and capable of striking back, should the North attack.

17 May 2017. The White House. President Donald J. Trump spoke with His Majesty King Abdullah II of Jordan to reaffirm the importance of close and continued cooperation between the United States and Jordan on a range of shared priorities.

17 May 2017, Sochi, Russia. Vladimir Putin held talks with Italian Prime Minister Paolo Gentiloni. Key aspects of bilateral cooperation and current international affairs were the main subjects of discussion.

17 May 2017. "I believe profoundly in the overhaul of the Europe," French President Emmanuel Macron told reporters last night, 17 May, before meeting with the European Council President Donald Tusk (60, from Poland), and stating he was "counting" on him for the revamp. "Europe needs your energy, imagination and courage," Donald Tusk responded. "Hope for a Europe that protects, wins, and looks to the future."

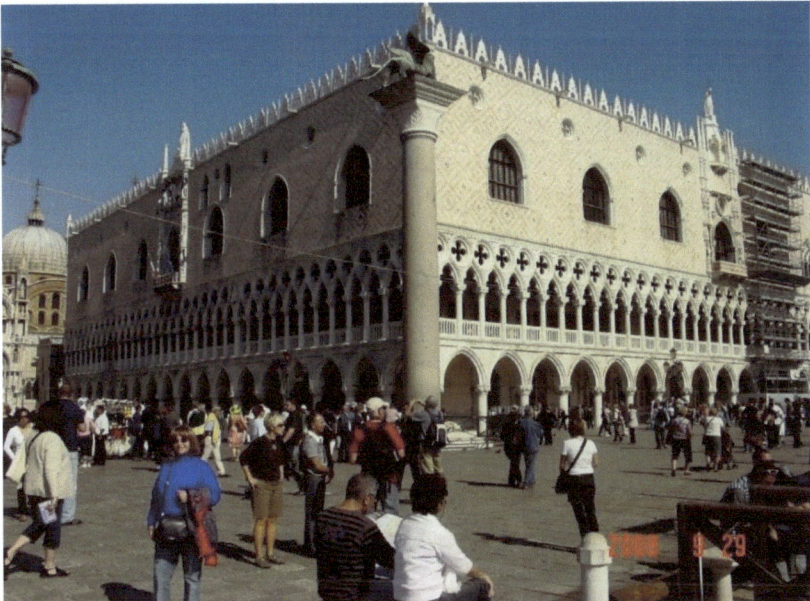

29 Sep 2008, Piazza San Marco (1084) looking northeast, Palazzo Ducale (1424), Basilica di San Marco (1173, left back), .Column of the Lion (center, with the sculpture Lion of Venice on top), Italy.

18 May 2017. Vladimir Putin had a telephone conversation with President of the French Republic Emmanuel Macron. Mr. Putin congratulated Mr. Macron on his official inauguration as French president, and on the new government's formation. The two presidents expressed a mutual desire to develop the traditionally

friendly ties between the two countries in politics, trade, the economy, cultural, humanitarian and other sectors. They also affirmed their desire to work together on current international and regional issues, including the fight against terrorism. In particular, they underscored the importance of continued cooperation within the Normandy format, to resolve Ukraine's internal conflict on the basis of the Minsk Agreements. Mr. Putin and Mr. Macron also discussed possibilities for upcoming personal contacts.

18 May 2017. At Venezuela's initiative, Vladimir Putin had a telephone conversation with President of the Bolivarian Republic of Venezuela Nicolas Maduro (54). Mr. Maduro briefed Mr. Putin on the internal political situation in Venezuela, and on measures taken to resolve the crisis. The Russian President wished the Venezuelan government success in their efforts to return the situation in the country to normal, and stressed the importance of resolving the current problems by acting within the law, and in accordance with Venezuela's legislation. The two presidents discussed current matters regarding the strategic partnership between the two countries, and implementation of mutually advantageous projects in various areas.

19 May 2017, from the White House: President Donald J. Trump met with President Juan Manuel Santos (65) of Colombia, to discuss ways to deepen the close friendship and longstanding partnership between the United States and Colombia.

19 May 2017. Xinhua. Any attempts to establish "two Chinas," "one China, one Taiwan," or "Taiwan independence" is doomed to fail, a spokesperson from the Chinese mainland said Thursday, 18 May 2017. An Fengshan, spokesperson for the Taiwan Affairs Office of the State Council, made the remarks in response to the name change of a Taiwan organization responsible for handling ties with Japan. A ceremony was held in Taiwan Wednesday, 17 May, announcing the change of name from the Association of East Asian Relations to Taiwan-Japan Relations Association.
An said the Foreign Ministry has already made its stance clear on this issue. "I want to stress that any attempts to create disturbances in the international arena or establish 'two Chinas,' 'one China, one

Taiwan,' or 'Taiwan independence' will be in vain and doomed to fail," An said. Foreign Ministry spokesperson Hua Chunying on Wednesday, 17 May, denounced the name change of the Taiwan organization, urging Japan to abide by the one-China policy, and not to disturb China-Japan ties.

20 May 2017. From White House. "President Donald J. Trump met today (20 May, in Saudi Arabia) with the Custodian of the Two Holy Mosques, King Salman bin Abd al-Aziz Al Saud (81) of Saudi Arabia, Crown Prince Mohamed bin Nayef (57) of Saudi Arabia, and Deputy Crown Prince Mohamed bin Salman (31) of Saudi Arabia. President Trump and King Salman signed a Joint Strategic Vision Statement, promising close collaboration to counter violent extremism, disrupt the financing of terrorism, and advance defense cooperation."

20 May 2017, from the White House. On Cuban Independence Day, I extend my warmest wishes to the Cuban American community, and the people of Cuba, as our whole Nation joins you in celebrating the anniversary of Cuban Independence. Americans and Cubans share allegiance to the principles of self-governance, dignity, and freedom.

20 May 2017. North Korea has successfully launched its second ballistic missile in a little more than a week (and the 11th missile it has fired this year).

20 May 2017, Xinhua. There is no space for ambiguity in the nature of cross-Strait relations, a Chinese mainland spokesperson said Friday, 19 May. Major changes have occurred to cross-Strait situation in the past year, resulting in increasing tensions in cross-Strait relations, the loss of past achievements in peaceful development of cross-Strait relations, and damages to the interests of compatriots on both sides of the Taiwan Strait, due to Taiwan authorities' refusal to accept the 1992 Consensus, which embodies the one-China principle, said An Fengshan, spokesperson for the Taiwan Affairs Office of the State Council. By refusing to endorse the 1992 Consensus, the Democratic Progressive Party (DPP) has undermined the common political foundation for the peaceful

development of cross-Strait relations. If the political foundation is damaged, cross-Strait relations will return to the old path of uncertainty and turmoil, An said. The fact that the Chinese mainland and Taiwan belong to one China shall not be changed, the principle of one China that is universally upheld by the international community shall not be challenged, he said. "We will unswervingly stick to the one-China principle, and uphold the 1992 Consensus. We will not tolerate any attempt to separate Taiwan from China," An said. Chinese people on both sides of the Strait should stand shoulder-to-shoulder to safeguard the foundation of cross-Strait relations, contain "Taiwan independence" forces, and endeavor to realize the great revival of the Chinese nation, An said.

20 May 2017. Iranian President Hassan Rouhani (68) won re-election by a wide margin Saturday, 20 May, getting an endorsement for efforts to seek better ties with the West, and attract more foreign investment.

21 May 2017. President Donald J. Trump delivered remarks at the Arab Islamic American Summit in Saudi Arabia. The President thanked King Salman and the Kingdom of Saudi Arabia for hosting the summit, and also thanked the many foreign leaders for attending (including from Qatar, Egypt, and Bahrain).

21 May 2017, Saudi Arabia, from the White House. President Donald J. Trump met today with President Abdel Fattah Al Sisi (62) of Egypt to build on their recent engagements, and continue efforts to strengthen the United States-Egypt strategic partnership.

21 May 2017, Xinhua. Xi Jinping, general secretary of the Communist Party of China (CPC) Central Committee, on Saturday, 20 May, congratulated Wu Den-yih (69) for being elected the chairperson of Kuomintang (KMT). Xi said in his message to Wu that he hoped the two parties shall keep in mind the well-being of the compatriots on both sides of the Taiwan Strait, adhere to the 1992 Consensus and firmly oppose "Taiwan independence." The CPC and KMT should stick to the correct direction for the peaceful

development of cross-Strait relations, and strive to achieve the great rejuvenation of the Chinese nation, Xi said.

In his reply to Xi's message, Wu expressed gratitude for Xi's congratulations, saying that he expected the two parties would continue to consolidate the 1992 Consensus, and promote the institutionalization of peace across the Strait. Wu expressed the hope that the two parties will carry forward the Chinese culture, advance sustainable development of both sides, and join each other on the road to a bright future.

Analysts say that the total size of the Federal Reserve's balance sheet was close to 0 (normal value) for over 60 years, until 1975, then began to grow fast, and exploded in 2008, now being around $4 T, because of the printing of dollars is done very fast (over $1,000/second).

22 May 2017, Paris. Promising to work on closer Eurozone ties in their first official meeting in Paris, Italian Prime Minister Paolo Gentiloni said Emmanuel Macron's election has been an "injection of trust and hope for Europe", and pushed for a common European migration policy. In turn, the French President called for a long-term roadmap to create a common euro area budget and strengthen European institutions.

22 May 2017, Riyadh, Saudi Arabia, from the White House: President Donald J. Trump met briefly today with President Ashraf Ghani of Afghanistan on the margins of the Islamic Summit in Riyadh, Saudi Arabia. President Trump welcomed President Ghani's leadership in Afghanistan on fighting terrorism and implementing key reforms. He also commended the brave service of Afghan security forces as they fight to secure their country.

22 May 2017. The 11 members of the TPP have agreed to pursue their trade deal without the U.S., at a forum of the Asia-Pacific Economic Cooperation.

23 May 2017. President Donald J. Trump has made it clear that under his Administration, the United States stands with Israel. The President spent Monday, 22 May, and Tuesday, 23 May 2017,

visiting Israel, strengthening the friendships and partnerships between our two countries. The President met with President Rivlin (77) and Prime Minister Netanyahu of Israel and visited several important sites.

23 May 2017. Bethlehem. President Donald J. Trump was warmly welcomed today in Bethlehem by President Mahmoud Abbas (82) of the Palestinian Authority. President Trump again stressed his belief that peace between Israelis and Palestinians is possible. President Trump and President Abbas reaffirmed their commitment to reach for a genuine and lasting peace between Palestinians and Israelis.

23 May 2017. Philippines President Rodrigo Duterte has declared martial law in the southern province of Mindanao, after Islamic State-aligned militants attacked Marawi, and raised the black IS flag at its town hall.

23 May 2017. Moscow. Vladimir Putin met with President of the Philippines Rodrigo Duterte, who has come to Russia on an official visit. Putin said: "I would like to begin our meeting by expressing condolences on the loss of Filipino lives in a terrorist attack. My colleagues and I understand that you need to get back home as soon as possible. I hope that the conflict you have mentioned will be settled without delay, with minimal losses."

23 May 2017. Moody's has lowered the China's credit rating to A1 from Aa3, citing Beijing's waning financial strength and rising liabilities. It marks the first time a major ratings agency has downgraded the country in more than 25 years. The move also received a backlash from China's finance ministry, which said the decision was "absolutely groundless" and was based on an "inappropriate calculation method."

24 May 2017. Rome. President Donald J. Trump today held meetings with Italian President Sergio Mattarella and Prime Minister Paolo Gentiloni. The leaders discussed the alliance between the United States and Italy, as well as priorities in the areas of defense cooperation, counterterrorism, and efforts to deny

terrorists safe havens from Mali to Libya to Iraq to Afghanistan. President Trump thanked Italy for its contributions to global counterterrorism efforts, especially its participation in the Global Coalition to Counter ISIS, and its active role in Iraq and Afghanistan. He also complimented Italy on its important diplomatic efforts to end the violence in Libya.

24 May 2017. President Donald J. Trump met today with His Holiness Pope Francis (80) and Cardinal Secretary of State Pietro Parolin (62). The Pope and the President discussed how religious communities can combat human suffering in crisis regions, such as Syria, Libya, and ISIS-controlled territory.
Upon completing their first meeting at the Vatican, Pope Francis gave President Trump a medal featuring an olive branch, a symbol of peace, among other gifts.

24 May 2017, Xinhua. Xi Jinping, general secretary of the Communist Party of China (CPC) Central Committee, has called both sides across the Taiwan Strait a community of shared destiny that cannot be prized apart.
Xi made the remarks in a congratulatory letter, made public Wednesday, 24 May, to the Association of Taiwan Investment Enterprises on the Mainland (ATIEM) on its 10th anniversary.
The Chinese mainland has gradually become a popular destination for Taiwan compatriots to invest, start businesses and make their home since the 1980s when the door between the two sides was reopened, Xi said.

24 May 2017. Moscow. Vladimir Putin met with President of the Republic of Macedonia Gjorge Ivanov (57), who is in Russia on a working visit. The two presidents discussed possibilities for furthering bilateral cooperation and exchanged views on current regional issues, especially the situation in the Balkans. Mr. Ivanov is in Russia to take part in a ceremony presenting him with the His Holiness Patriarch Alexis II Prize, awarded by the public organization International Foundation for the Unity of Orthodox Christian Nations.

25 May 2017. Brussels, Belgium. President Donald J. Trump hosted French President Emmanuel Macron for a working lunch today at the official residence of the United States Ambassador to Belgium. The meeting marked the first in-person engagement between the two presidents, and follows on their initial telephone call on May 9.

In advance of the NATO Leaders Meeting, President Trump urged President Macron to meet the NATO defense spending pledge and ensure that NATO is focused on counterterrorism. The President thanked President Macron for France's leadership in counterterrorism efforts in Africa. The leaders agreed on the critical importance of defeating ISIS in Iraq and Syria. President Trump discussed his recent travel to Saudi Arabia and Israel and his hope for Middle East peace. The two leaders committed to maintaining and building on the already strong alliance between the United States and France as they cooperate on these and other vital issues.

25 May 2017. Brussels, Belgium. Yesterday, 24 May, President Donald J. Trump visited the Royal Palace in Brussels to meet with King Philippe (57) and Queen Mathilde (44), and with Prime Minister Charles Michel (41) of Belgium. This visit marked the President's first engagement with Belgian leadership. At the Royal Palace, President Trump and the First Lady first met with the King and Queen and expressed their appreciation for the hospitality and their long personal support for better economic relations between Belgium and the United States. This year is the centennial year of the Commission for Relief in Belgium, which kept millions of Belgians from starving during World War I and currently supports Belgian educational exchanges with the United States.

In a subsequent meeting with Prime Minister Charles Michel, the President praised Belgian contributions to the Global Coalition to Counter ISIS, noting the critical importance of Belgian F-16s flying missions in Iraq and Syria. On the eve of the NATO Leaders Meeting, the President discussed the responsibility of all nations to share our common defense burden, including the need for all NATO members to meet the Wales commitment to spend 2% of their Gross Domestic Product on defense.

25 May 2017. Brussels, Belgium.   President Donald J. Trump met today in Brussels with European Council President Donald Tusk and European Commission President Jean-Claude Juncker. The leaders reaffirmed the strong bond between the United States and Europe, anchored in shared values and longstanding friendship.

25 May 2017. From the White House. The United States condemns the recent violence perpetrated by an ISIS-linked terrorist group in the southern Philippines. These cowardly terrorists killed Philippine law enforcement officials and endangered the lives of innocent citizens. The United States will continue to provide support and assistance to Philippine counterterrorism efforts. The United States is a proud ally of the Philippines, and we will continue to work with the Philippines to address shared threats to the peace and security of our countries.

25 May 2017. The USS Dewey has sailed within 12 nautical miles of an artificial Chinese island in the South China Sea, according to reports, marking the first such challenge to Beijing since President Trump took office. The patrol, known as a freedom of navigation operation, is designed to keep critical sea lanes and strategic waters open in the Pacific Ocean.

25 May 2017. BBC sources say the U.K. has stopped sharing intelligence with the U.S. after leaks regarding the Manchester terrorist attack. At least 22 people were killed and 59 more injured in the blast that occurred outside Manchester Arena right after the end of a concert late Monday 22 May, night (UK time).

25 May 2017, Xinhua. Chinese President Xi Jinping on Wednesday, 24 May, called for efforts to build the People's Liberation Army (PLA) Navy into a strong and modern force to lend support for the realization of the Chinese dream of national rejuvenation, and the dream of a strong army.
Xi, who is also general secretary of the Communist Party of China (CPC) Central Committee and chairman of the Central Military Commission (CMC), made the remarks during an inspection of the PLA Navy headquarters. The navy must resolutely safeguard the

CPC Central Committee's authority and unwaveringly stick to the Party's absolute leadership, Xi stressed.

26 May 2017. Taormina, Italy. President Donald J. Trump met today with Prime Minister Shinzo Abe of Japan in Taormina, Italy, before the start of the G7 Summit. In the wake of the horrific terrorist attack at the Manchester Arena in the United Kingdom, the two leaders reaffirmed their shared resolve to cooperate to the fullest extent possible to counter terrorist threats.
The President said the United States will work with Japan and the Republic of Korea, as well as our other allies and partners around the world, to increase pressure on North Korea and demonstrate that North Korea's current path is not sustainable. President Trump and Prime Minister Abe agreed their teams would cooperate to enhance sanctions on North Korea, including by identifying and sanctioning entities that support North Korea's ballistic missile and nuclear programs. They also agreed to further strengthen the alliance between the United States and Japan, to further each country's capability to deter and defend against threats from North Korea.

26 May 2017, from official Chinese article. Chinese navy missile frigates identified and expelled a U.S. destroyer entering the South China Sea on May 25, the Ministry of National Defense (MOD) confirmed the same day.
MOD spokesman Colonel Ren Guoqiang told a routine press briefing that the USS Dewey entered waters adjacent to the Meiji Reef, prompting the PLA Navy missile frigates CNS Liuzhou and CNS Luzhou to identify and warn it to leave the area.
He reaffirmed that China has "indisputable sovereignty" over the Nansha Islands and waters surrounding them. "The Chinese military lodged solemn representations with the United States against such acts of flaunting its forces and boosting regional militarization."
The MOD spokesman stressed that the United States is a destabilizing factor.

27 May 2017. From an official article. China has developed a new type of ultrafast anti-missile interceptor capable of knocking down an incoming projectile that is flying 10 times faster than a bullet, according to the nation's largest missile maker.

China Aerospace Science and Industry Corp, one of the major defense contractors for the People's Liberation Army, recently revealed that its Second Academy in Beijing has made a "new-generation aerospace defense missile" that incorporates top space technologies, and which it describes as one of the cornerstones of a world power's strategic prowess.

28 May 2017. Xinhua. China strongly denounced the communique released after a G7 (USA, UK, France, Japan, Germany, Italy, Canada, EU (8th)) summit, saying it interfered in the East China Sea and South China Sea issues in the guise of international law, Foreign Ministry spokesperson Lu Kang said early Sunday, 28 May.

The 2017 G7 summit concluded with a joint communique Saturday, 27 May, saying the G7 members are committed to "maintaining a rules-based order in the maritime domain based on the principles of international law", and expressing concerns about the situation in the East China Sea and South China Sea.

28 May 2017. China Daily. China denied US allegations that two Chinese fighter jets unsafely intercepted a US military plane earlier this week, saying that its aircraft were acting in accordance with the law.

"Related remarks from the US side are inconsistent with fact," Wu Qian, a spokesman for the Defense Ministry, said on Sunday, 28 May. "The Chinese aircraft investigated the US plane in accordance with the law, and related maneuvers were professional and safe."

"Recently, US military has frequently dispatched planes and ships into China's sea and air territory, threatening our sovereignty and security, as well as putting the lives of front-line staff in danger," he added.

On May 25, two Chinese J-10 fighter jets came within 182 meters of a P-3 Orion surveillance plane flying 240 kilometers south east of Hong Kong. One of the jets flew in front of the US aircraft, "restricting its ability to maneuver," according to foreign media, citing anonymous US military officials.

On the same day, the USS Dewey, a US guided missile destroyer, was sailing near a group of islands in the Nansha Islands in the South China Sea. The People's Liberation Army Navy dispatched two frigates, the Liuzhou and Luzhou, to investigate and warn the US ship to leave.

On May 17, the WC-135 Constant Phoenix - a US reconnaissance aircraft - was carrying out operation in airspace over the Chinese Yellow Sea, and Chinese aircraft acted to identify and investigate in accordance with the law," the statement said, calling the action "professional" and "safe", according to ministry's previous statements.

"These actions are the root cause of the security issue between China and the US, both in the air and at sea," Wu said. "We again urge the US to take concrete actions to correct and avoid such incidents from happening again."

"The Chinese military will resolutely carry out its duty, and protect national sovereignty and security," he added.

29 May 2017. Palace of Versailles, France. Russian President Vladimir Putin (64.5) met with President of France, Emmanuel Macron (39.4), at the Palace of Versailles. Mr. Putin is in France on a working visit at Mr. Macron invitation.

29 May 2017, Versailles, France. French President Macron: "During the presidential election, France made a sovereign affirmation of its commitment to independence, its European choice, and its desire to influence the fate of the world. None of the major challenges these days can be tackled without a dialogue with Russia."

Russian President Putin: "However, today, we spent more time discussing our bilateral relations, and relations between Russia and the European Union. We spoke about the problem spots in the world, and looked together for common approaches to resolving these complicated matters."

Vladimir Putin and French President Emmanuel Macron toured the exhibition Peter the Great (1672-1725, aged 52.5): A Tsar in France, 1717 (Tsar was 45), at the Grand Trianon of the National Museum of the Palace of Versailles.

29 May 2017, Seoul — North Korea launched a ballistic missile on Monday 29 May, which flew 450 Km miles and landed

in Japan's so-called exclusive economic zone, the South Korean military and the Japanese government said.

President Moon Jae-in of South Korea called a Security Council meeting for later Monday morning to discuss the launch, and Japan's cabinet secretary condemned the launch, coming a week after the North last tested a ballistic missile, as a provocation.

The United States Pacific Command said in a statement that a short-range ballistic missile was tracked from North Korea for six minutes, before it landed in the Sea of Japan.

30 May 2017. The Kremlin, Moscow, Russia. Vladimir Putin received Mohammad bin Salman Al Saud (31), Deputy Crown Prince, Second Deputy Chairman of the Ministers' Council and Defense Minister of Saudi Arabia, at the Kremlin. The discussion covered the countries' cooperation to stabilize the global oil market, and the situation in Syria.

30 May 2017, Xinhua. Germany's top diplomat Sigmar Gabriel on Monday, 29 May, released harsh words on the United States, saying U.S. President Donald Trump's policies have weakened the West. "The short-sighted policies of the American government stand against the interests of the European Union. The West has become smaller, at least it has become weaker," Gabriel said. The German foreign minister referred to the G7 meeting and the NATO summit last week, noting that Trump's performance was unsatisfactory, since he refused to endorse NATO's collective defense principles. "Anyone who sells more weapons in conflict areas, and who does not want to politically resolve religious conflicts, is putting Europe's peace at risk," Gabriel said.

Gabriel made the remarks on the sidelines of a round-table discussion on migrant crisis in Berlin.

His words also echoed German Chancellor Merkel's "beer tent speech" a day before, when Merkel also cast doubts on Europe's alignment with the United States and Britain.

Merkel, during a campaign in Germany's southern state of Bavaria, said following the election of Trump and Brexit, Europeans "really have to take destiny into their own hands."

Spiegel Online, an influential German news hub, dubbed the words of the two politicians as "a trans-Atlantic turning point," saying their speech clearly want to distance Germany from Trump.

30 May 2017. Xinhua. South Korean President Moon Jae-in on Tuesday, 30 May, ordered an investigation into the unauthorized delivery of four more mobile launchers of the U.S. missile shield to the country. Yoon Young-chan, chief presidential press secretary, told a press briefing that President Moon said it was "very shocking" after he was briefed, by his top national security advisor Chung Eui-yong, on the unauthorized delivery. About two weeks before the May 9 presidential election, two mobile launchers and a radar, for the U.S. Terminal High Altitude Area Defense (THAAD) missile interception system, were transported in the middle of night to a golf course at Soseong-ri village in Seongju county, North Gyeongsang province. THAAD is composed of six mobile launchers, 48 interceptors, an AN/TPY-2 radar, and a fire and control unit.

30 May 2017. China's foreign ministry has again called for THAAD to be removed from South Korea, after the U.S. missile defense system was installed in the country. It's also making waves since South Korea's new leader was not told about THAAD's latest deployment.

31 May 2017, from the White House. President Donald J. Trump called President Ashraf Ghani of Afghanistan to convey his deepest condolences to the families and friends of those killed and injured in the murderous attack that took place this morning near the diplomatic zone in Kabul.

An international team of researchers has discovered that a microRNA, produced by certain white blood cells, can prevent excessive inflammation in the intestine.

USA, Chicago 1837: Willoughby Tower (1929, 38 fl, 134 m, right), Chicago Athletic Association Bldg., Anno Domini 1891, center.

6 April 1978, Pisa, Cattedrale di Pisa (1092, striped-marble, left), Torre di Pisa (August 1173-1372, 55.86 m on the low side, 56.67 m on the high side, white-marble, 296 steps, right).

Chapter 6. June 2017

1 June 2017, from the White House. The US President met with the Prime Minister Nguyen Xuan Phuc (62.8) of Vietnam. As a Pacific power with widespread interests and commitments throughout the Asia Pacific, the United States shares many important interests with Vietnam. The two leaders emphasized that many opportunities lie ahead for United States-Vietnam relations, including increasingly enhanced political, diplomatic, economic and trade ties, and ever-growing cooperation in the areas of science and technology, national defense and security, education, people-to-people exchange, humanitarian and war legacy issues, as well as regional and international issues of mutual concern.

1 June 2017, from the White House. Today, President Donald J. Trump announced that the United States will withdraw from the Paris Climate Accord, and begin negotiations to either re-enter or negotiate an entirely new agreement with more favorable terms for the United States. The Paris Climate Accord cost the U.S. economy nearly $3 trillion in reduced output, over 6 millions of industrial jobs, and over 3 millions of manufacturing jobs.

1 June 2017. France, Germany and. Italy regret President Trump's decision to withdraw from the Paris climate accord, dismissing his suggestion that the pact could be revised. "This agreement is less about the climate and more about other countries gaining a financial advantage over the U.S.," Trump said from the Rose Garden, at the White House.

1 June 2017, from the White House. President Donald J. Trump spoke by telephone today with President Emmanuel Macron of France, Chancellor Angela Merkel of Germany, Prime Minister Justin Trudeau of Canada, and Prime Minister Theresa May of the United Kingdom. The President personally explained his decision to withdraw the United States from the Paris Climate Accord. He thanked all four leaders for holding frank, substantive discussions on this issue during his first months in office.

1 June 2017, St Petersburg, Russia. Russian President Vladimir Putin met with Prime Minister of India Narendra Modi (66) on the sidelines of the St Petersburg International Economic Forum.

2 June 2017. The US national debt is over $19.93 T, and is increasing by over $10,000/second. The debt ceiling (normal it should be 0), now is $20 T.

2 June 2017, St Petersburg, Russia. Vladimir Putin had a meeting with UN Secretary-General Antonio Guterres on the sidelines of the St Petersburg International Economic Forum.
The UN Secretary-General mentioned: "Recently, we have been observing some disturbing trends: phenomena such as xenophobia, racism, and also irrational behavior, including the isolationist approach adopted by certain states. One reason why the multilateral approach is so important is, in fact, the existence of areas of instability."

2 June 2017, St Petersburg, Russia. Russian President Vladimir Putin met with Federal Chancellor of Austria, Christian Kern.

2 June 2017, St Petersburg, Russia. Russian President Vladimir Putin met with Vice Chancellor, Minister of Foreign Affairs of the Federal Republic of Germany, Sigmar Gabriel.

2 June 2017, St Petersburg, Russia. Russian President Vladimir Putin met with President of Moldova, Igor Dodon.

3 June 2017. From the White House. President Donald J. Trump spoke with Prime Minister Theresa May of the United Kingdom today. The President offered his condolences for the brutal terrorist attacks on June 3 in central London.

5 June 2017. Four Arab states have cut off diplomatic ties with Qatar, as well as closing air and sea routes, pointing to Doha's ties to terrorism. The coordinated move by Saudi Arabia, Egypt, the

UAE and Bahrain marks a sharp escalation of a rift between the Persian Gulf states since late last month.

5 June 2017. At Turkey's initiative, Russian President Vladimir Putin had a telephone conversation with President of the Republic of Turkey, Recep Tayyip Erdogan. The two presidents discussed the developments around Qatar, and called on all interested countries to engage in dialogue with a view to reaching a compromise, for the sake of preserving peace and stability in the Persian Gulf area.

5 June 2017. Official Chinese article. The Chinese Ministry of National Defense (MOD) denied late on June 5 that one People's Liberation Army (PLA) helicopter violated Indian airspace. The MOD made the statement in response to Indian media allegations.

6 June 2017. From the White House. President Donald J. Trump spoke today with the Custodian of the Two Holy Mosques, King Salman bin Abdulaziz Al Saud of Saudi Arabia. The two leaders discussed the critical goals of preventing the financing of terrorist organizations and eliminating the promotion of extremism by any nation in the region.

6 June 2017. From the White House. The United States military continued a number of airstrikes, and two raids against al-Qa'ida in the Arabian Peninsula (AQAP) operatives and facilities.

6 June 2017. From the White House. Combat-equipped forces, deployed since January 2002 to the Naval Base, Guantánamo Bay, Cuba, continue to conduct humane and secure detention operations for detainees held at Guantánamo Bay under the authority provided by the 2001 Authorization for the Use of Military Force, as informed by the law of war. There were 41 such detainees as of the date of this report.

6 June 2017. From the White House. United States forces, including strike and combat support aircraft with associated United States military personnel, remain deployed to Turkey to support

defeat-ISIS operations, and to support the defense of Turkey, at the Turkish government's request.

6 June 2017. From the White House. The Force Management Level for U.S. Armed Forces in Afghanistan currently is 8,448.

6 June 2017. From the White House. The Force Management Level for U.S. Armed Forces in Iraq currently is 5,262.

6 June 2017. From the White House. The Force Management Level for U.S. Armed Forces in Syria is 503. As I previously reported, on April 6, 2017, at my direction, United States forces in the Mediterranean Sea, operating beyond the territorial sea of any state, struck the Shayrat military airfield in Syria.

6 June 2017. From the White House. Approximately 700 military personnel are assigned to, or supporting the United States contingent of the Multinational Force and Observers, which have been present in Egypt since 1981.

6 June 2017. At Russia's initiative, Vladimir Putin had a telephone conversation with President of the Arab Republic of Egypt Abdel Fattah el-Sisi. The two presidents discussed in detail the further development of bilateral cooperation in different areas, and the crises in the Middle East and North Africa.

6 June 2017. Russian President Vladimir Putin had a telephone conversation with Emir of Qatar Tamim bin Hamad Al Thani (37).

Research and development spending by U.S. businesses has begun increasing robustly, as the economic recovery has continued, reaching an all-time high of $499 billion in 2015—the most spent by any nation in a single year. And the business sector's share of those outlays rose to a record $344 B, which represents 69% of all business and non-buisness related research and development spending.

7 June 2017. White House. President Donald J. Trump spoke today with Crown Prince Mohamed bin Zayed Al Nahyan (56) of the United Arab Emirates. (Vice President Pence is 59 today).

7 June 2017. White House. President Donald J. Trump spoke today with Amir Sheikh Tameem bin Hamad Al Thani of Qatar.

8 June 2017. Vladimir Putin met in Astana with President of the People's Republic of China Xi Jinping. The two presidents discussed current bilateral cooperation matters.

8 June 2017. Xinhua. "China and Kazakhstan, friendly neighbors bound by mountains and rivers, have been committed to consolidating our political mutual trust, strengthening cooperation in all areas, and promoting our coordination in international and regional issues since they established diplomatic relations 25 years ago," President Xi noted.
"The booming China-Kazakhstan relationship has brought concrete benefits to the two countries and their peoples," he said. "I look forward to engaging in deep-going exchanges with my old friend, President Nursultan Nazarbayev, and chart the course of our bilateral relations together."

8 June 2017. Xinhua. Chinese President Xi Jinping and his Afghan counterpart, Mohammad Ashraf Ghani, pledged on Thursday, 8 June, to boost bilateral cooperation within the framework of the Belt and Road (B&R) Initiative.
The two heads of state made the remarks during their meeting in Astana, capital of Kazakhstan. Xi arrived here Wednesday evening for a state visit to Kazakhstan and the 17th meeting of the Council of Heads of State of the Shanghai Cooperation Organization (SCO). Hailing the good momentum of bilateral ties, Xi said that high-level interaction should play an important role in guiding China-Afghanistan relations and that exchanges on all levels should be intensified.
Xi voiced the hope that the two sides will actively implement their memorandum of understanding on jointly promoting the B&R construction and other related deals, deepen bilateral practical cooperation, and carry out connectivity projects between them.

For his part, Ghani said Afghanistan cherishes the friendship with China, and is grateful for China's help in its peaceful reconstruction and reconciliation process.

The Afghan president said his country values China's important role in international and regional affairs, and is committed to closer economic, trade and security cooperation.

Afghanistan is highly appreciative of the B&R Initiative and looks forward to aligning its own development with the B&R construction, Ghani said, adding that his country will actively participate in cooperation on transport connectivity.

8 June 2017. Xinhua. China has resolutely opposed the latest U.S. military report that distorts China's legitimate development in military and security sectors and is meant to spread the so-called "military threat from China".

The U.S. Department of Defense recently published its Annual Report to Congress on Military and Security Developments Involving the People's Republic of China 2017.

The report summarized the developments in the People's Liberation Army (PLA) organizational reform, highlighted China's new weapon's capabilities, China's regional maritime claims, and presented its interpretation of the situation across the Taiwan Strait.

8 June 2017. A day after Seoul said it would postpone full deployment of U.S. anti-missile system THAAD, whose installation is controversial in the region, North Korea fired a salvo of cruise missiles off its east coast. The launch comes less than a week after the U.S. Security Council passed fresh sanctions against Pyongyang, as punishment for its missile tests.

9 June 2017. White House. The U. S. President met at the White House with Romanian President Klaus Iohannis (58 on June 13), and he said "thank you for being here. It's an honor to welcome such a good friend of America to the White House."

9 June 2017, White House. President Donald J. Trump spoke today with Prime Minister Theresa May of the United Kingdom, to offer his warm support regarding the election.

9 June 2017. White House. President Donald J. Trump spoke today with President Abdel Fattah Al Sisi of Egypt. The two presidents agreed on the importance of all countries implementing the agreements reached in Riyadh to fight terrorism, counter extremism, and stop the funding of terrorist groups. President Trump also emphasized the importance of maintaining unity among Arab countries.

9 June 2017. The Shanghai Cooperation Organization (SCO) summit agenda includes current issues of the SCO activities, the anti-terrorist efforts, the Middle East situation and the decision to grant India and Pakistan the status of full members in the organization. The SCO Summit has resulted in the adoption of a series of documents, including the Astana Declaration, which outlines the consolidated approaches of the SCO member-states to the development of the organization and their positions on the key international issues; the Convention on Counteracting Extremism, the Statement of the SCO Heads of State on the Joint Counteraction of International Terrorism, and others. The summit participants also approved the membership of India and Pakistan in the Shanghai Cooperation Organization.

The event was attended by delegation heads of the SCO observer states: President of the Islamic Republic of Afghanistan Ashraf Ghani, President of the Republic of Belarus Alexander Lukashenko, Prime Minister of the Republic of India Narendra Modi, President of Mongolia Tsakhiagiin Elbegdorj (54), Prime Minister of the Islamic Republic of Pakistan Nawaz Sharif (67), and Minister of Foreign Affairs of the Islamic Republic of Iran Mohammad Javad Zarif (57). United Nations Secretary-General Antonio Guterres, Chairman of the Executive Committee and Executive Secretary of the Commonwealth of Independent States Sergei Lebedev, Deputy Secretary General of the Collective Security Treaty Organization Amanzhol Zhankuliyev, Secretary-General of the Association of Southeast Asian Nations Le Luong Minh, and Executive Director of the Conference on Interaction and Confidence-Building Measures in Asia Jianwei Gong, also attended the meeting.

"China supports the SCO in speaking with one voice on international and regional issues," Xi said.

The President of Russia arrived in Kazakhstan the day before. He has met with President of the People's Republic of China Xi Jinping, who is also attending the SCO Summit, to discuss current bilateral and international issues, including the preparations for the Chinese leader's upcoming visit to Russia.

9 June 2017. Xinhua.   Chinese President Xi Jinping met Friday, 9 June, in Astana, capital of Kazakhstan, with Indian Prime Minister Narendra Modi, calling for closer cooperation between the two countries.
Hailing the long-lasting friendship between the two countries with ancient civilizations, Modi said a sound India-China relationship will help stabilize the volatile international situation.
The Indian side is grateful for China's support for India's accession to the SCO and will work closely with China in the organization, Modi said.

9 June 2017. Astana, Kazakhstan. Vladimir Putin met with President of Mongolia, Tsakhiagiin Elbegdorj. The two leaders met after the SCO summit to discuss bilateral cooperation.
Vladimir Putin met with Pakistani Prime Minister Nawaz Sharif on the sidelines of the SCO Summit.

13 June 2017. Russian President Vladimir Putin had a telephone conversation with King of Saudi Arabia Salman bin Abdulaziz Al Saud. Taking into account the results of Deputy Crown Prince of Saudi Arabia, Mohammad bin Salman Al Saud's recent visit to Moscow, the President of Russia and the King of Saudi Arabia discussed current issues of further developing Russian-Saudi relations in various areas and expressed a mutual commitment to intensifying bilateral cooperation.

13 June 2017. At the UAE's initiative, Russian President Vladimir Putin had a telephone conversation with Crown Prince of Abu Dhabi and Deputy Supreme Commander of the Armed Forces of the United Arab Emirates Mohammed Al Nahyan (56).
During a discussion of the aggravation of tensions around Qatar, which is worsening the already grave situation in the entire Middle East, mutual interest in defusing the crisis was expressed.

13 June 2017. Xinhua. Xi Jinping, chairman of the Central Military Commission (CMC), has conferred an honorary title on a unit from the People's Liberation Army (PLA) Hong Kong Garrison. In a military order issued recently, Xi told PLA troops to follow the example set by the company and to spare no efforts in building a strong army.

14 June 2017. Xinhua. Chinese President Xi Jinping said Wednesday, 14 June, that China expects that Luxembourg will play an active role in developing relations between China and the European Union (EU). Xi made the remarks during a meeting with visiting Luxembourg Prime Minister Xavier Bettel (44), saying that he hopes Luxembourg can push the EU to provide more favorable conditions for the development of China-EU cooperation.
For his part, Bettel said his visit to China aims to promote the in-depth development of bilateral cooperation. (Trump is 71).

15 June 2017. Xinhua. Chinese President Xi Jinping (64 today) met with FIFA president Gianni Infantino (47, from Switzerland) on Wednesday, 14 June, at the Great Hall of the People in the heart of Beijing. Xi, an avid European football fan, noted that the Chinese government attached great significance to the development of football and provided strong and consistent support for the sport, although China lagged far behind traditional football powerhouses for years, in terms of both the sport's domestic popularity, and competence on the terrain.
"We can really start a new era of football, not only in China, President Xi, but in the whole world, because we are really passionate about football," said Infantino.

16 June 2017. White House. President Donald J. Trump spoke today with Prime Minister Justin Trudeau of Canada to address various aspects of the strong bilateral relationship between their two countries. President Trump commended Prime Minister Trudeau for Canada's recent announcement that it will increase military spending by 70% over the next decade. President Trump underscored the solid alliance that the United States enjoys with Canada.

16 June 2017. White House. President Donald J. Trump spoke today with President Pedro Pablo Kuczynski of Peru to discuss bilateral and regional issues. President Trump discussed with President Kuczynski the new United States policy on Cuba.

16 June 2017. From the White House. President Donald J. Trump is changing the policy of the United States toward Cuba to achieve four objectives:
1- Enhance compliance with United States law—in particular the provisions that govern the embargo of Cuba and the ban on tourism;
2- Hold the Cuban regime accountable for oppression and human rights abuses ignored under the Obama policy;
3- Further the national security and foreign policy interests of the United States and those of the Cuban people; and
4- Lay the groundwork for empowering the Cuban people to develop greater economic and political liberty.

16 June 2017. White House. Statement from President Donald J. Trump on the Passing of Helmut Kohl.
On behalf of the American people, I offer my deepest condolences to the people of Germany and to the family and loved ones of former Chancellor Helmut Kohl. We were saddened to learn of his passing today in Ludwigshafen, his boyhood home.

17 June 2017. Vladimir Putin sent a message of condolence to President of Germany, Frank-Walter Steinmeier, and Federal Chancellor of Germany, Angela Merkel, on the death of Helmut Kohl (1930-2017, 87 years old), a highly esteemed statesman and one of the patriarchs of European and world politics.

19 June 2017. Xinhua. Chinese President Xi Jinping said Monday, 19 June, that BRICS cooperation would be more productive, and usher in a new "golden decade."
Xi made the remarks when meeting with the heads of delegations from Brazil, Russia, India and South Africa, who are in Beijing to attend the BRICS foreign ministers' meeting.

The five countries' share in the global economy increased from 12% to 23% in the past decade, while contributing to more than half of global growth.

19 June 2017. White House. President Donald J. Trump today met with President Juan Carlos Varela of Panama (53), and discussed the close ties and longstanding partnership between the United States and Panama.

19 June 2017. An American warplane shot down a Syrian army jet on Sunday, 17 June, marking the first such occurrence in the country's years-long civil war.

20 June 2017. Analysts say that the threat of direct Russian-American confrontation in Syria is escalating. Moscow said it would treat any plane from the U.S.-led coalition flying west of the Euphrates River as a potential "aerial target", and suspended communications via a military hotline. It comes after the U.S. downing of a Syrian government jet over the weekend.

20 June 2017. White House. President Donald J. Trump met today with President Petro Poroshenko of Ukraine to discuss support for the peaceful resolution to the conflict in eastern Ukraine, and President Poroshenko's reform agenda and anticorruption efforts.

20 June 2017. "While I greatly appreciate the efforts of President Xi & China to help with North Korea, it has not worked out. At least I know China tried!" President Trump wrote in a tweet. It follows the death of 22-year-old Otto Warmbier, whom Pyongyang held for more than a year.

20 June 2017. Russian President Vladimir Putin held talks in the Kremlin with President of Kyrgyzstan, Almazbek Atambayev, who is in Russia on a state visit.

20 June 2017. Xinhua. Chinese President Xi Jinping Tuesday underscored centralized and unified leadership to boost integrated military and civilian development.

Xi, also general secretary of the Communist Party of China (CPC) Central Committee and chairman of the Central Military Commission, made the remarks at the first plenary meeting of the central commission for integrated military and civilian development, which he heads.

20 June 2017. Russian President Vladimir Putin had a telephone conversation with President of the Republic of Bulgaria, Rumen Radev (54, general), at the Bulgarian side's initiative.
The two presidents affirmed their mutual interest in developing Russian-Bulgarian cooperation in different areas, including energy.

21 June 2017. White House. President Donald J. Trump spoke today with Crown Prince Mohamed bin Salman of Saudi Arabia to congratulate him on his recent elevation.

21 June 2017. Russian President Vladimir Putin met at the Kremlin with President of the Federative Republic of Brazil, Michel Temer (76), who is in Russia on an official visit.
The two presidents discussed the full range of Russian-Brazilian relations. They gave particular attention to developing and diversifying trade and economic ties, and strengthening cultural and humanitarian cooperation. They also exchanged views on key regional and international issues.
A number of bilateral documents were signed following the talks.

21 June 2017. North Korea has carried out another test of a rocket engine that the U.S. believes could be part of its program to develop an intercontinental ballistic missile. The news comes a day after Secretary of State Rex Tillerson urged China, Pyongyang's sole ally, to put more pressure on the North to rein in its atomic weapons and ballistic missile programs.

23 June 2017. Article in China Daily. Chinese State Councilor Yang Jiechi (67) co-chaired a diplomatic and security dialogue with U.S. Secretary of State Rex Tillerson, and Secretary of Defense James Mattis (66); Fang Fenghui (66), a member of China's Central Military Commission (CMC) and chief of the CMC

Joint Staff Department, also participated in the dialogue in Washington D.C., the United States, on June 21, 2017.
The Korean Peninsula, the South China Sea, terrorism, military-to-military cooperation, and other issues were discussed. .

24 June 2017. Xinhua. Chinese President Xi Jinping has called for comprehensively improving the country's rocket launch and test capabilities. Xi, who is also general secretary of the Communist Party of China (CPC) Central Committee and chairman of the Central Military Commission (CMC), made the remarks during inspection of a space force unit based in Shanxi Province in north China on Thursday.

25 June 2017. White House. Statement from the Press Secretary on the Terrorist Attacks in Pakistan. The United States strongly condemns the terrorist attacks in Parachinar and Quetta on Friday, 23 June. These attacks, which deliberately targeted civilians, and killed over 80 people, are a strong reminder of the threat posed throughout the region by the scourge of terrorism. We stand with the people of Pakistan in their fight against it.

26 June 2017. White House. President Donald J. Trump hosted Prime Minister Narendra Modi of India at the White House on June 26 for an official visit to Washington, D.C.

26 June 2017. White House. Statement from President Donald J. Trump. Today's unanimous Supreme Court decision is a clear victory for our national security. It allows the travel suspension for the six terrorism-prone countries, and the refugee suspension, to become largely effective.

26 June 2017. Escalating a trade dispute ahead of NAFTA negotiations, the U.S. Commerce Department has imposed preliminary anti-dumping duties on Canadian softwood lumber. Combined with the preliminary anti-subsidy duties imposed in April, total duties on the key construction material will range from 17.41% to 30.88%.

27 June 2017. White House. President Donald J. Trump spoke today with President Emmanuel Macron of France, to congratulate the French people on France's successful parliamentary elections. President Trump complimented President Macron for his leadership of the new political party that secured a majority in the French National Assembly, and wished him luck in launching his legislative agenda.

27 June 2017. Xinhua. China urges India to immediately withdraw its border guards that have crossed the boundary, and have a thorough investigation of this matter, a Chinese Foreign Ministry spokesperson said Monday, 26 June, night.
According to spokesperson Geng Shuang, Indian border guards crossed the boundary in the Sikkim section of the China-India border and entered the territory of China, and obstructed normal activities of Chinese frontier forces in the Donglang area recently, and the Chinese side has taken counter-measures.

27 June 2017. Business leaders, academics and politicians have gathered in the Chinese port of Dalian for the World Economic Forum's annual June meeting. The theme for the gathering, also known as the "Summer Davos," will be innovation, with the focus on companies from the developing world.

27 June 2017. Reuters. Japanese and EU negotiators meeting in Tokyo press ahead with a free trade deal that aims to counter U.S. protectionism.

27 June 2017. Bahrain has accused Qatar of a "military escalation" in the crisis that has embroiled the region, warning there would be consequences, after Turkey deployed additional troops to its base in Qatar.

28 June 2017. Xinhua. President Xi Jinping said the non-governmental forum of the Conference on Interaction and Confidence-Building Measures in Asia (CICA) will contribute to regional peace and stability, and common prosperity.
(CICA Member States: Afghanistan, Azerbaijan, Bahrain, Bangladesh, Cambodia, China, Egypt, India, Iran, Iraq, Israel,

Jordan, Kazakhstan, Kyrgyzstan, Mongolia, Pakistan, Palestine, Qatar, Republic of Korea, Russia, Tajikistan, Thailand, Turkey, United Arab Emirates, Uzbekistan, Viet Nam.
Observers:
(i) States: Belarus, Indonesia, Japan, Laos, Malaysia, Philippines, Sri Lanka, Ukraine and USA
(ii) Organizations: International Organization for Migration(IOM), League of Arab States, Organization for Security and Cooperation in Europe (OSCE), Parliamentary Assembly of the Turkic Speaking Countries (TURKPA) and United Nations.)
The non-governmental forum was established based on a proposal by Xi at the Shanghai Summit of the CICA in May 2014.

29 June 2017. Vladimir Putin met in the Kremlin with President of the Socialist Republic of Vietnam, Tran Dai Quang (60), who is in Russia on an official visit.
On the agenda were ways to further deepen the comprehensive strategic partnership between the two countries.

29 June 2017. At Russia's initiative, Vladimir Putin had a telephone conversation with President of Turkmenistan Gurbanguly Berdimuhamedov (60).
The two presidents discussed key aspects of bilateral relations and their further development in the political, trade, economic, cultural and humanitarian spheres, and also examined efforts to strengthen security and stability in Central Asia and the Caspian region.

29 June 2017. Vladimir Putin met at the Kremlin with German Vice Chancellor and Foreign Minister, Sigmar Gabriel, to discuss various aspects of Russian-German relations.

29 June 2017. Vladimir Putin received American political expert and former US secretary of state, Henry Kissinger (94), at the Kremlin. Henry Kissinger is in Russia to attend the Primakov Readings International Forum.

29 June 2017. Xinhua. Hong Kong. President Xi Jinping set foot on Hong Kong Thursday 29 June.

Xi, also general secretary of the Communist Party of China (CPC) Central Committee, and chairman of the Central Military Commission, is here to attend celebrations marking the 20th anniversary of Hong Kong's return to the motherland, and the inauguration of the fifth-term government of the Hong Kong Special Administrative Region (HKSAR).

He will also inspect the special administrative region.

This is Xi's first trip to Hong Kong as Chinese president.

30 June 2017. White House. President Trump and President Moon of the Republic of Korea had a bilateral meeting regarding North Korea, and renegotiating a trade deal.

Built on mutual trust and shared values of freedom, democracy, human rights, and the rule of law, the United States-ROK partnership has never been stronger, and the two leaders pledged to build an even greater Alliance going forward.

30 June 2017. White House. President Donald J. Trump spoke today with President Recep Tayyip Erdogan of Turkey about numerous subjects, including ways to resolve the ongoing dispute between Qatar and its Gulf and Arab neighbors, while ensuring that all countries work to stop terrorist funding, and to combat extremist ideology.

30 June 2017. At the initiative of the German side, Vladimir Putin had a telephone conversation with Federal Chancellor of the Federal Republic of Germany, Angela Merkel. In anticipation of the G20 (USA, China, Russia, UK, France, India, Japan, Germany, Italy, Canada, Australia, Brazil, South Korea, Turkey, Saudi Arabia, Argentina, Indonesia, Mexico, South Africa, Europe) Summit to be held in Hamburg on July 7–8, the leaders discussed the main items on the forum's agenda. They also spoke about the Paris Agreement, and issues of bilateral cooperation.

30 June 2017. Vladimir Putin had a telephone conversation with President of Turkey Recep Tayyip Erdogan. The discussion focused on key aspects of the Syrian settlement, in light of the upcoming fifth International Meeting on Syria in Astana, convened under the aegis of Russia, Turkey and Iran, in the beginning of July.

30 June 2017. Xinhua. Hong Kong. President Xi Jinping on Friday, 30 June, inspected the Chinese People's Liberation Army (PLA) Garrison in the Hong Kong Special Administrative Region (HKSAR) at Shek Kong barracks, on the eve of the 20th anniversary of Hong Kong's return to China.

Xi, also general secretary of the Central Committee of the Communist Party of China, and chairman of the Central Military Commission, reviewed the troops in the company of Tan Benhong, commander of the PLA Garrison in the HKSAR.

More than 3,100 officers and soldiers took part in the review, and over 100 pieces of military equipment, including air defense missiles and helicopters, were displayed.

30 June 2017. China official article. The Ministry of National Defense (MOD) has once again demanded India remove troops trespassing across the border in the Sikkim section, and obstructing Chinese border guards' normal activities.

The MOD spokesperson confirmed that PLA's new tanks were being tested in a high-altitude environment in Tibet. However, he rebuffed allegations that linked the tank with recent border tensions with India, saying the tests targeted no country.

Researchers at Memorial Sloan Kettering Cancer Center in New York have discovered that bacteria living in the gut provide a first line of defense against severe Listeria infections.

Use of statins may speed up the onset of Parkinson's disease symptoms in people who are susceptible to the disease, according to Penn State College of Medicine researchers.

Household tasks performed by children lead to happy children, however surveys show that less than 30% of parents require their children to perform household tasks.

Japan: Mount Fuji (3,776 m, 1707 last eruption), seen from 17 km north in Kawaguchiko (Lake Kawaguchi, 6 km^2, 830 m elevation).

Chapter 7. July 2017

1 July 2017. Vladimir Putin had a telephone conversation with Emir of the State of Qatar, Tamim bin Hamad Al Thani (37), at the Qatari side's initiative. The two leaders discussed the crisis in relations between Qatar and a number of other states. Vladimir Putin stressed the importance of political and diplomatic efforts aimed at overcoming the disagreements and normalizing the current complicated situation.

1 July 2017. Vladimir Putin had a telephone conversation with King of Bahrain, Hamad bin Isa Al Khalifa (67), at the Bahraini side's initiative.

1 July 2017. Hong Kong. Xinhua. President Xi Jinping Saturday, 1 July, drew the "red line" for handling relations between the mainland and Hong Kong, warning against attempts to undermine national sovereignty or challenge the central government's power. "Any attempt to endanger national sovereignty and security, challenge the power of the central government and the authority of the Basic Law of the HKSAR, or use Hong Kong to carry out infiltration and sabotage activities against the mainland is an act that crosses the red line, and is absolutely impermissible," he said.

1 July 2017. Xinhua. The 15th East Asia Forum was held Friday in central China's Hunan Province, discussing the construction of East Asia economic community among other major agendas. The forum focused on reviewing 20 years of APT (ASEAN (Association of Southeast Asian Nations (10): Vietnam, Cambodia, Laos, Thailand, Myanmar, Malaysia, Singapore, Indonesia, Philippines, Brunei) Plus Three (China, Japan, South Korea)) cooperation, motivating small and medium-sized enterprises in regional integration, and formulating a blueprint for the East Asia economic community. Nearly 100 officials, entrepreneurs and scholars from ASEAN countries plus China, Japan and the Republic of Korea (10+3), as well as representatives from the ASEAN

Secretariat, attended the event in Changsha, provincial capital of Hunan.

2 July 2017. White House. President Donald J. Trump spoke this evening with Prime Minister Shinzo Abe of Japan. The two leaders exchanged views on the growing threat from North Korea, including their unity with respect to increasing pressure on the regime to change its dangerous path.

2 July 2017. White House. President Donald J. Trump spoke separately today with King Salman bin Abdulaziz Al Saud of Saudi Arabia, Crown Prince Mohamed bin Zayed Al Nahyan of Abu Dhabi, and Emir Tamin bin Hamad Al Thani of Qatar. On the calls, President Trump addressed his concerns about the ongoing dispute between Qatar, and some of its Gulf and Arab neighbors.

2 July 2017. China Daily. China lashed out at the United States over the Trump administration's approval of a Taiwan arms deal, with the authorities demanding the US stop the sales. The Trump administration had notified the US Congress of "seven proposed defense sales for Taiwan" worth about $1.42 billion. The arms sales, the first such deal with Taiwan since Donald Trump took office as US president, will go forward unless the US Congress formally objects in the next 30 days, according to the Associated Press.
China, having lodged solemn representations to the US in both Beijing and Washington, "strongly urges" the country to revoke the arms sales, and cut military contacts with Taiwan, to avoid further damaging China-US ties, and cooperation in important fields, Foreign Ministry spokesman Lu Kang said on Friday.
The arms sales would be a grave violation of the principles of the three joint communiques between China and the US, and damage China's sovereignty and security interests, Lu said. They also run counter to the spirit of the important consensus that the two countries' heads of state reached in their meeting in Florida in April, and are not in line with the general trend of the development of bilateral ties or the US's own interests, Lu pointed out.
Ren Guoqiang, spokesman for the Ministry of National Defense, said: "China is resolutely opposed to arms sales to Taiwan by the

government of any foreign country." "The position of the Chinese military over safeguarding China's sovereignty and territorial integrity is firm and clear," Ren said. The revelation of the arms deal came one day after a US Senate committee completed a markup of a bill, allowing the US Navy to make regular port calls in Taiwan. This drew an immediate protest from China.

Ma Xiaoguang, spokesman of the Taiwan Affairs Office of the State Council, warned on Friday, 30 June: "Any behavior of relying on foreign forces to magnify oneself, and damage peace and stability across the Taiwan Straits, will surely backfire."

Cui Tiankai, Chinese ambassador to the US, told reporters on the sidelines of a reception at the Chinese embassy on Thursday, 29 June, the arms deal "will certainly undermine the mutual confidence between the two sides".

2 July 2017 evening. White House. President Donald J. Trump spoke today with President Xi Jinping of China. President Trump raised the growing threat posed by North Korea's nuclear and ballistic missile programs. Both leaders reaffirmed their commitment to a denuclearized Korean Peninsula. President Trump reiterated his determination to seek more balanced trade relations with America's trading partners

3 July 2017. Xinhua. China said on Sunday, 2 July, that the U.S. missile destroyer trespassing China's territorial waters off the Xisha Islands was "serious political and military provocation."

Foreign Ministry spokesperson Lu Kang said in a statement released on Sunday night that China dispatched military vessels and fighter planes in response, to warn off the U.S. vessel.

Earlier Sunday, the missile destroyer USS Stethem trespassed China's territorial waters off the Xisha Islands.

The Xisha Islands are an inherent part of the Chinese territory, Lu said, noting that in accordance with the Law of the People's Republic of China on the Territorial Sea and the Contiguous Zone, the Chinese government promulgated the baseline of the territorial sea off the Xisha Islands in 1996.

3 July 2017 morning China time. The same telephone conversation described above, on 2 July evening Washington time,

is now presented by Chinese Xinhua. Chinese President Xi Jinping and his U.S. counterpart Donald Trump held a telephone conversation on Monday, 3 July morning, exchanging views on bilateral ties, the upcoming G20 summit, and the Korean Peninsula issue. During the conversation, Xi stressed that important results have been achieved in bilateral relations between China and the United States since the Mar-a-Lago meeting between the two heads of state. Meanwhile, China-U.S. relations have also been affected by some negative factors, and the Chinese side has already expressed its position to the United States, Xi said.

The Chinese president also said that his country attaches great importance to Trump's reaffirmation that the United States will adhere to the one-China policy.

China hopes that the United States will handle the Taiwan issue appropriately, in accordance with the one-China principle, and the three China-U.S. joint communiques, Xi said.

Xi stressed that both China and the United States need to control the general direction of bilateral relationship, in light of the consensus they reached at the Mar-a-Lago meeting. The two sides should also stick to the principle of mutual respect and mutual benefit, focus on cooperation, and control differences, in a bid to secure more substantial progress in relations between the two countries, Xi added. Trump, for his part, said that the U.S.-China ties have a promising prospect, and the two countries have broad common interests. Trump reaffirmed that the U.S. government will continue to honor the one-China policy, and its stance remains unchanged.

The two presidents also discussed the peace and stability of the Korean Peninsula. They agreed to meet in Hamburg to discuss issues of common concern.

3 July 2017. Xinhua. The turmoil in Syria has brought a lot of suffering to its people and grave challenges to regional and world peace, Chinese President Xi Jinping has said.

In an interview with Russian media published Monday, 3 July, Xi stressed that the only way out of this would be a political solution.

"China's position on the Syrian issue has been consistent," said Xi. "Syria's sovereignty and territorial integrity should be protected and respected, and its future decided by its own people." "A political solution offers the only way out," said the Chinese president.

Xi expressed an appreciation for Russia's important and active role in trying to reach a proper solution to the Syrian issue.

3 July 2017. Xinhua. The U.S. deployment of an advanced anti-missile system in South Korea gravely harms the strategic security interests of China, Russia and other countries in the region, Chinese President Xi Jinping has said.

In an interview with Russian media published Monday, Xi pointed out that the Terminal High Altitude Area Defense (THAAD) installation jeopardizes the strategic balance in the region and is unhelpful to denuclearizing the Korean Peninsula and maintaining regional peace and stability. China and Russia have kept close communication and coordination at various levels on the issue, and hold very similar views on its essence and damage, said Xi, whose country has unequivocally rejected the move.

He added that Beijing and Moscow are steadfastly opposed to the THAAD deployment and seriously suggest that relevant countries stop and cancel the installation. The two countries, he said, will take necessary measures, jointly or individually, to safeguard their national security interests and the regional strategic balance.

3 July 2017 morning. Xinhua. Chinese President Xi Jinping reiterated on Monday, 3 July, that China-Russia relations are at their "best time in history," saying the two nations are each other's most trustworthy strategic partners. Xi made the remarks during an interview with Russian media, ahead of his state visit to Russia.

3 July 2017 evening. The Kremlin, Moscow. Vladimir Putin (64.8) met in the Kremlin with President of the People's Republic of China Xi Jinping (64), who has come to Russia on a two-day official visit. The main talks are scheduled for July 4. During the top-level talks the parties are expected to discuss a whole range of issues pertaining to comprehensive partnership and strategic cooperation between Russia and China, as well as current international and regional problems. Following the talks, a number of bilateral documents will be signed.

4 July 2017. White House. President Donald J. Trump spoke today with Prime Minister Paolo Gentiloni of Italy, to discuss the

agenda for the upcoming G20 Summit in Hamburg, Germany, and to renew his appreciation for the Prime Minister's efforts in hosting the exceptional G7 Summit in May.

4 July 2017. The Kremlin, Moscow. Vladimir Putin and President of China Xi Jinping, who has come to Russia on an official visit at the invitation of the Russian President, met for talks in the Kremlin. During the restricted format talks, the participants discussed political, trade and economic, military-technical, and humanitarian cooperation between the two countries. During the consultations, attended by delegation members, the in-depth discussion of the agenda continued.

Before the expanded talks, the President of Russia presented to the President of China the Order of St Andrew the Apostle.

Also, as part of the Chinese President's official visit to Russia, Vladimir Putin and Xi Jinping met with representatives of public organizations, and the business and media communities of the two countries.

Based on the results of the Chinese President's visit to Russia, Vladimir Putin and Xi Jinping signed a Joint Statement of the Russian Federation and the People's Republic of China on the Further Expansion of Comprehensive Partnership and Strategic Cooperation, and a Joint Statement of the Russian Federation and the People's Republic of China on the Current Status of Global Affairs and Important International Issues. Moreover, the two leaders approved an Action Plan to implement the Treaty on Good-Neighborliness, Friendship and Cooperation between the Russian Federation and the People's Republic of China for 2017–2020.

4 July 2017. Xinhua. Visiting Chinese President Xi Jinping and his Russian counterpart, Vladimir Putin, met Monday, 3 July, and agreed to further cement bilateral ties and strengthen coordination on the Korean Peninsula, and other major issues.

China and Russia are comprehensive strategic partners of coordination, and it is quite important for them to intensify communication and coordination in dealing with major affairs, said Xi, who had a tete-a-tete with Putin in the Kremlin shortly after his arrival in Moscow. The two leaders also exchanged views on the Korean Peninsula and Syria issues. They agreed to jointly push for a proper settlement of the peninsula issue via dialogue and negotiation. As for the U.S. deployment of the Terminal High Altitude Area Defense (THAAD) system in South Korea, Xi and Putin said the move concerns the strategic balance in the region.

China and Russia, they stressed, are both opposed to installing THAAD in South Korea.

Russia is the first leg of Xi's ongoing foreign trip, which will also take him to Germany for a state visit, and the upcoming summit of the Group of 20 major economies.

4 July 2017. The U.S. has confirmed that North Korea's latest launch was indeed an intercontinental ballistic missile, calling it a "new escalation of threat," as North Korea vowed to keep sending the U. S. more "gift packages". Calling for global action, the U.S. has requested an emergency meeting of the U.N. Security Council, while South Korea seeks fresh sanctions on North Korea.

4 July 2017. Analysts noticed that China launched Asia's biggest, and most advanced warship, as China strengthens naval presence

5 July 2017. The White House. President Donald J. Trump spoke today aboard Air Force One with President Abdel Fattah Al Sisi of Egypt, to address the ongoing dispute between Qatar and its Arab neighbors.

5 July 2017. Xinhua. Visiting Chinese President Xi Jinping met on Tuesday, 4 July, with German Chancellor Angela Merkel, saying his country supports the European Union (EU) to be "united, stable, prosperous and open."

The meeting was held at the Max Liebermann Haus (Max Liebermann House) nearby Brandenburg Gate in Berlin.

6 July 2017. President Trump delivered remarks in Poland saying, "I declare today for the world to hear that the West will never, ever be broken. Our values will prevail. Our people will thrive. And our civilization will triumph. So, together, let us all fight like the Poles - for family, for freedom, for country, and for God."

6 July 2017. The White House. President Donald J. Trump met today in Warsaw with President Kolinda Grabar-Kitarovic (49) of Croatia to discuss issues of mutual interest, and ways to further deepen already strong United States-Croatia relations.

6 July 2017. Russian President Putin had a telephone conversation with President of Kazakhstan Nursultan Nazarbayev. The two leaders discussed the resolution of the Syrian crisis, taking into account the results of the 5th International Meeting on Syria, which took place in Astana on July 4–5.

6 July 2017. Poland has agreed to buy Patriot missile defense systems from the U.S., in a deal worth up to $7.6 B, as President Trump visited Warsaw to discuss transatlantic relations.

6 July 2017. The White House President Donald J. Trump met in Hamburg, Germany, today, with Chancellor Angela Merkel of Germany, to coordinate on key policy areas ahead of tomorrow's G20 Summit.

6 July 2017. Before the start of the G20 Summit in Hamburg, Germany, an informal meeting took place between the heads of state and government of the BRICS countries (Brazil, Russia, India, China and South Africa).

6 July 2017. Xinhua Chinese President Xi Jinping arrived in the northern German city of Hamburg Thursday for the 12th Group of 20 (G20) Summit.

6 July 2017. Vladimir Putin had a telephone conversation with Prime Minister of Israel Benjamin Netanyahu, at the Israeli side's initiative.

6 July 2017. The European Union and Japan are to sign a major free trade deal today in Brussels, ahead of this weekend's G20 summit in Hamburg.

6 July 2017. Xinhua. The Indian troops are currently in Chinese territory, and the matter remains unsettled," Chinese

Foreign Ministry spokesperson Geng Shuang said at a routine press briefing. He urged India to show sincerity in resolving border disputes and developing bilateral ties, and create conditions for the normal development of China-India relations.

6 July 2017. Xinhua. China on Thursday, 6 July, accused India of taking the protection of Bhutan as an excuse to legitimize its border incursion into China.

7 July 2017. The White House President Donald J. Trump, President Moon Jae-in, and Prime Minister Shinzo Abe met in Hamburg, Germany, on July 6, to discuss the serious and escalating threat posed by the nuclear and ballistic missile programs of the Democratic People's Republic of Korea (DPRK).

Military analysts present the full force of the North Korean army. There are plenty of heavy machines in the North Korean military. According to a Newsweek analysis, North Korea has 3,500 tanks, 72 submarines, 302 helicopters, 563 combat aircraft, and 21,100 pieces of artillery. North Korea has one of the largest militaries in the world. Missiles aside, one of North Korea's most formidable assets may be the sheer size of its military. Because the country has universal conscription, North Korea's military has 1.19 million active members, and another 7.7 millions in reserve. The official policy is tanks yes, cars no. Only military and government officials are allowed to own motor vehicles in the country. South Korea has discovered four tunnels under the DMZ -- apparent attempts by North Korea to create an invasion route. The first tunnel, discovered in 1974, had already been fortified with concrete, wired with electricity and equipped with a narrow railway capable of transferring 20,000 soldiers per hour. Today, these "tunnels of aggression" are guarded by the South Korean military, and are available for visit by tourists.

7 July 2017. The White House. President Donald J. Trump met today with President Enrique Peña Nieto of Mexico during the G20 Summit in Hamburg, Germany.

7 July 2017. Xinhua Chinese President Xi Jinping said Thursday, 6 July, that China and Singapore shall grasp the bilateral relations with strategic insight and vision, and keep mutual understanding and support on issues of each other's core interests and major concerns. Xi made the remarks while meeting with Singaporean Prime Minister Lee Hsien Loong (65) in Hamburg, Germany.

7 July 2017. A meeting between Russian President Vladimir Putin and Prime Minister of Japan Shinzo Abe took place on the sidelines of the G20 summit in Hamburg, Germany.

7 July 2017. China.org. The 2017 China-Central and Eastern European Countries (CEEC) Political Parties Dialogue will be convened in Bucharest, Romania, in mid-July.
Around 400 political party leaders and entrepreneurs from China and CEEC will gather and discuss issues related to the China-proposed Belt and Road Initiative.

8 July 2017. The White House. President Trump had a bilateral meeting with President Xi of China, at the G20 Summit in Hamburg, Germany. Both sides reaffirmed their commitment to a denuclearized Korean Peninsula.
Xinhua: Xi told Trump that stronger China-U.S. ties are conducive to stability and prosperity, and serve the interests of both peoples and the international community, in a complex world, where various conflicts emerge. For his part, Trump hailed the "wonderful relationship" with Xi, and expressed confidence in the "success" of addressing common problems together with China.
In Florida, the two presidents spent more than seven hours in in-depth discussions, gained better understanding of each other, cemented mutual trust, reached consensus on many major issues, and built up a good working relationship.

8 July 2017, Xinhua. U.S President Donald Trump (71) and Russian President Vladimir Putin (64.8) on Friday, 7 July, agreed on a ceasefire in Syria, at the ongoing G20 summit in Hamburg, Germany, according to local media Focus Online.

The ceasefire is to take effect on July 9 at noon Damascus time, sources close to the delegations said. No further details were disclosed.

The two leaders talked for over two hours, longer than scheduled.

8 July 2017. The White House. President Trump had a bilateral meeting with Prime Minister May of the United Kingdom, during the G20 Summit in Hamburg, Germany.

8 July 2017. The White House. President Trump and Prime Minister Abe of Japan had a bilateral meeting at the G20 Summit in Hamburg, Germany.

8 July 2017. The White House. President Trump and President Widodo of Indonesia had a bilateral meeting at the G20 Summit in Hamburg, Germany.

8 July 2017. The White House. President Trump and Prime Minister Lee Hsien Loong of Singapore had a bilateral meeting at the G20 Summit in Hamburg, Germany.

8 July 2017. Vladimir Putin began the second day of the G20 Summit with a working breakfast with Federal Chancellor of Germany Angela Merkel, and President of France Emmanuel Macron. The leaders discussed the situation in Ukraine, and ways to settle the crisis.

Later Vladimir Putin had meetings with President of Turkey Recep Tayyip Erdogan, President of the European Commission Jean-Claude Juncker, and a separate bilateral meeting with Emmanuel Macron.

The previous evening, the Russian leader also held brief contacts with Prime Minister of the Netherlands Mark Rutte (50), Prime Minister of Italy Paolo Gentiloni, Prime Minister of Norway Erna Solberg (56), Prime Minister of Vietnam Nguyen Xuan Phuc, and UN Secretary General Antonio Guterres.

8 July 2017, Xinhua. Chinese President Xi Jinping met with Japanese Prime Minister Shinzo Abe on bilateral ties, on the

sidelines of the ongoing Group of 20 (G20) summit on Saturday, 8 July, in Hamburg, Germany.

8 July 2017. Russian President Vladimir Putin congratulated Khaltmaa Battulga (54) on his election as President of Mongolia.

8 July 2017, Xinhua. Chinese President Xi Jinping on Friday 7 July, called on members of the Group of 20 (G20) major economies, to champion an open world economy, and a multilateral trade regime, as global growth remains unsteady despite signs of recovery.

8 July 2017. G20 concluded: "We will continue to fight protectionism including all unfair trade practices," G20 leaders declared in a joint communique on Saturday, 8 July, following a meeting in Hamburg, Germany. However, the group stepped back from an unequivocal commitment to free trade for the first time since its inaugural summit in 2008. Instead, it said it would "strive to ensure a level playing field," noting "the importance of reciprocal and mutually advantageous trade and investment frameworks."

9 July 2017. Xinhua. Chinese President Xi Jinping and his French counterpart, Emmanuel Macron, agreed on Saturday, 8 July, to promote bilateral relations and cooperation.

9 July 2017. Xinhua. President Xi Jinping on Friday, 7 July, met with British Prime Minister Theresa May amid the Group of 20 (G20) summit, calling for more stable, rapid and sound development of bilateral relations. May said that Britain is committed to boosting the global comprehensive strategic partnership for the 21st century between the two countries, and sticking to the general direction of the "Golden Era" of bilateral relations.

9 July 2017. During his visit to Yekaterinburg, Russian President Vladimir Putin met with Former Japanese Prime Minister, now President of the Organizing Committee of the Tokyo 2020 Olympic Games, Yoshiro Mori (80). Vladimir Putin invited Yoshiro Mori for an informal dinner, to discuss the state of the two countries' relations, and prospects for their further development.

9 July 2017. Xinhua. . The Hamburg summit G20 took place. The violent protests, that rocked the streets of the German port city, have also reflected that, while globalization has helped generate unprecedented prosperity worldwide, a more inclusive global economic growth now seems to be a more pressing priority.

For the past week, whether at Moscow and Berlin for state visits, or in Hamburg for the G20 gathering, Chinese President Xi Jinping has demonstrated China's readiness to join the rest of the world in building a better world for everyone.

In his meeting with South Korean President Moon Jae-in, Xi urged Seoul to listen to China's major concerns, and clear the hurdles in bilateral ties, referring to the former South Korean government's decision to let THAAD in.

"Those who work alone, add; those who work together, multiply," Xi quoted a German proverb as saying.

"In this spirit, let us work together to promote interconnected growth for shared prosperity, and build toward a global community with a shared future," added the president.

10 July 2017. Iraq has declared a week-long holiday to mark the victory. The country has fully defeated Islamic State in Mosul, three years after the militants seized the city, and made it the stronghold of their self-proclaimed caliphate. "I announce from here the end, and the failure, and the collapse of the terrorist state of falsehood and terrorism," Prime Minister Haider al-Abadi (65) said on state television.

10 July 2017. The White House. Statement from President Donald J. Trump on the Liberation of Mosul.
Today, Iraqi Security Forces, supported by the United States and the Global Coalition, liberated the city of Mosul from its long nightmare under the rule of ISIS. We congratulate Prime Minister Haider al-Abadi, the Iraqi Security Forces, and all Iraqis for their victory over terrorists, who are the enemies of all civilized people.

11 July 2017. The White House. President Donald J. Trump spoke today with Prime Minister Haider al-Abadi of Iraq. President Trump congratulated the Prime Minister on the liberation of Mosul

by Iraqi Security Forces, which marks a major milestone in the fight against ISIS.

12 July 2017. President Trump will travel to Paris today to meet with Emmanuel Macron. He'll be the guest of honor at Bastille Day (14 July) events - a celebration of French national pride at a time when, according to Macron, "our world has never been so divided." The two leaders will look for common ground on terrorism and defense policy.

12 July 2017. Xinhua. Ships carrying Chinese military personnel departed Zhanjiang in southern China's Guangdong Province on Tuesday, 11 July, to set up a support military base in Djibouti.

12 July 2017. Russian President Vladimir Putin had a telephone conversation with Venezuelan President Nicolas Maduro, at the initiative of the Venezuelan side.
The presidents exchanged views on a number of practical issues of Russian-Venezuelan cooperation, in particular, the implementation of mutually beneficial joint projects in the fuel and energy sector.
Mr. Maduro informed Mr. Putin on the Venezuelan government's efforts to normalize the domestic political situation in the country.

12 July 2017. While they appreciate the "U.S. efforts," sanctions against Qatar will continue until demands of the four Arab states leading the boycott are met, according to Saudi Arabia, the UAE, Egypt, and Bahrain.

12 July 2017. The U.S. State Department has approved a possible $3.9 B Patriot system sale to Romania, in a move likely to anger Russia. Vladimir Putin has said his country will be forced to enhance its own missile strike capability in response.

13 July 2017. The White House. President Donald J. Trump was deeply saddened to learn of the passing of Nobel Peace Prize laureate and prominent Chinese political prisoner Liu Xiaobo (61, died under guard in a Chinese hospital). The President's heartfelt condolences go out to Liu Xiaobo's wife, Liu Xia, and his family

and friends. A poet, scholar, and courageous advocate, Liu Xiaobo dedicated his life to the pursuit of democracy and liberty.

13 July 2017. Vladimir Putin had a telephone conversation with King Abdullah II of the Hashemite Kingdom of Jordan, at the Jordanian side's initiative.

The discussion focused on current situation in the Middle East, primarily in the context of the common efforts to fight international terrorism. Special mention was made of the importance of the memorandum on the creation of a de-escalation zone in southwest Syria, signed by Russia, Jordan and the United States in Amman, on July 7, 2017, with the intention of further working toward ceasefire in other regions of the Syrian Arab Republic as well.

14 July 2017. The White House. Statement from President Donald J. Trump on Bastille Day 2017.

The ties between the United States and France stretch back almost as far as our shared history as democratic republics. France is America's first and oldest ally. In 1778, our two countries signed a treaty of friendship and alliance. We have remained joined in common purpose ever since.

France was instrumental in the United States winning its independence. More than a century later, American doughboys repaid the debt. On July 4, 1917, at the tomb of the great French hero of the American Revolution, an American army officer crystalized his country's gratitude with the immortal words, "Lafayette (1757-1834), we are here."

On behalf of the American people, we congratulate the people of France, and look forward to many more centuries of friendship and cooperation.

14 July 2017. The White House. President Donald J. Trump spoke today from Air Force One with King Salman bin Abdulaziz Al Saud of Saudi Arabia. King Salman congratulated President Trump on the victory over ISIS in Mosul.

14 July 2017. Vladimir Putin congratulated President of France, Emmanuel Macron, on the French national holiday, Bastille Day.

"Relations between Russia and France date back centuries, as we were reminded when we opened together the exhibition at the Versailles Palace to mark 300 years since the visit by Emperor Peter the Great to France. Historical events of this kind are indicative of the special nature of relations between our countries, and of mutual respect and sympathy between our people," the Russian President wrote in his message.

14 July 2017. Real monthly federal spending topped $400 B for the first time in June, when the Treasury spent a record $429 B, according to the most recent Monthly Treasury Statement. As the Treasury was spending the record figure, it was taking in approximately $339 B in taxes - thus, running a deficit for the month of $90 B.

14 July 2017. The White House. President Donald J. Trump Proclaims July 16 through July 22, 2017, as Captive Nations Week
CAPTIVE NATIONS WEEK, 2017
BY THE PRESIDENT OF THE UNITED STATES OF AMERICA
A PROCLAMATION
During Captive Nations Week, we stand in solidarity with those living under repressive regimes, and we commit to promoting our American ideals, grounded in respect for natural rights and protected by the rule of law, throughout the world.
The Soviet Union collapsed more than a quarter of a century ago, but hundreds of millions of people around the world still live under the tyranny of authoritarian regimes.
We continue to encourage despotic regimes to turn away from their oppressive ideologies and embrace a more hopeful and prosperous future for their people. This week, and always, we stand with all people throughout the world who are fighting for liberty, justice, and the rule of law.

15 July 2017, Xinhua. The Communist Party of China (CPC) Friday issued a revised regulation on inspection, in a renewed effort to improve supervision and governance of its more than 89 millions of members. The inspections should staunchly safeguard the authority and the centralized, unified leadership of the CPC Central Committee, with Comrade Xi Jinping as the core, and ensure the

CPC is always the firm and core leadership of the socialist cause with Chinese characteristics.

15 July 2017. Xinhua. The Belt and Road (B&R) Exhibition opened in Bucharest on July 14, 2017, on the sidelines of the 2017 China-CEE Countries Political Parties Dialogue held in the Romanian capital.

17 July 2017. The White House. Yesterday, the Venezuelan people again made clear that they stand for democracy, freedom, and rule of law. Yet their strong and courageous actions continue to be ignored by a bad leader who dreams of becoming a dictator.

17 July 2017. A major once-in-five-years Chinese government work meeting indicated China was looking to increase control over the economy.

18 July 2017. The White House. President Donald J. Trump spoke today with Sultan Qaboos bin Sa'id Al Sa'id (76) of Oman. President Trump underscored the importance of close bilateral cooperation.

18 July 2017. Xinhua. China supports a political settlement of the Palestinian issue on the basis of the two-state solution, President Xi Jinping said Tuesday, 18 July.
China supports Palestine in building an independent, full sovereignty state along the 1967 borders, with East Jerusalem as its capital, Xi said in his talks with visiting Palestinian President Mahmoud Abbas.
China will unswervingly push forward relations with Palestine, and the Middle East peace process, Xi said.
Prior to the talks, Xi held a red-carpet welcome ceremony for Abbas at the Great Hall of the People in Beijing. Abbas is on a state visit to China from July 17 to 20, at the invitation of Xi.

20 July 2017. Xinhua. Chinese President Xi Jinping has called on the country's major military research and educational institutions, to cultivate more talent for the armed forces, and to build world-class military research and educational institutions.

"It takes first-class military talent, theory, and science and technology to build the PLA into a world-leading military," Xi said. "Science and technology is the core fighting capacity in modern warfare," he noted.

20 July 2017. Germany and Turkey have traded insults, and threatened economic retaliation, after the detention of a German human-rights activist, sent already stormy relations into a downward spiral.

21 July 2017, Xinhua. China is looking to recruit more college students for its armed forces in 2017.

21 July 2017. Vladimir Putin had a meeting with President of Azerbaijan, Ilham Aliyev (55), in Sochi, Russia.

21 July 2017. Military talks aimed at easing tensions between the two Koreas failed to take place today, after the North disregarded a call from Seoul. The discussions would have marked the first official such talks since December 2015. South Korea President Moon Jae-in took office in May, pledging to engage Pyongyang in dialogue.

23 July 2017. Chinese GTN. A Chinese naval fleet reached Russia's Baltic city of Kaliningrad on July 21, 2017, ready for a joint drill with Russia, scheduled in the Baltic Sea in late July.

24 July 2017. As per prior agreement, Vladimir Putin had a telephone conversation with Chancellor of Germany Angela Merkel, President of the French Republic Emmanuel Macron, and President of Ukraine Petro Poroshenko, in the Normandy format.
The four leaders heard reports by OSCE Special Monitoring Mission Chief Monitor, Ertugrul Apakan, and Principal Deputy Chief Monitor, Alexander Hug, about maintaining the ceasefire on the line of contact between the parties to the internal Ukrainian conflict, and also about other aspects of OSCE SMM activity.
After that, the leaders exchanged opinions on the situation in southeast Ukraine, in light of serious violations of the Minsk Agreements that were signed on February 12, 2015.

Vladimir Putin spoke in detail about Russia's approach to the key provisions of the Minsk Agreements. The four leaders have agreed to maintain contact, including at the top level.

24 July 2017. The White House. The U.S. Drug Interdiction Assistance will continue to the Government of Colombia.

24 July 2017. Household debt has reached an all-time high in the U.S., according to the Federal Reserve Bank of New York.

25 July 2017. The White House. President Trump and Prime Minister Hariri (47) of Lebanon had a bilateral meeting.
The President and Prime Minister discussed topics such as the importance of defeating terrorist organizations like ISIS and Al Qaeda. The President commended the Lebanese people for "standing up for humanity in a very troubled part of the world." The meeting aimed to strengthen the two country's relationship in order to ensure stability, mutual prosperity, and peace.

25 July 2017. St. Petersburg. Vladimir Putin met in St Petersburg with Vice President of Iraq, Nouri al-Maliki (67), who is in Russia on a working visit, to discuss bilateral cooperation, and the situation in the Middle East.

25 July 2017. The 2017 BRICS Youth Forum themed "Enhance BRICS Partnership, Promote Youth Development" kicked off in Beijing on July 25.
A total of 50 young delegates including politicians, experts, business leaders and students from the BRICS countries (Brazil, Russia, India, China and South Africa) attended the three-day event hosted by the All-China Youth Federation (ACYF).

26 July 2017. The White House. President Donald J. Trump Proclaims July 27, 2017, as National Korean War Veterans Armistice Day.
On National Korean War Veterans Armistice Day, we honor the patriots who defended the Korean Peninsula against the spread of Communism in what became the first major conflict of the Cold

War. We remember those who laid down their lives in defense of liberty, in a land far from home, and we vow to preserve their legacy. Situated between World War II and the Vietnam War, the Korean War has often been labeled as the "Forgotten War," despite its having claimed the lives of more than 36,000 Americans. The Korean War began on June 25, 1950, when North Korean forces, backed by the Soviet Union, invaded South Korea. Shortly thereafter, American troops arrived and pushed back the North Koreans. For 3 years, alongside fifteen allies and partners, we fought an unrelenting war of attrition. Through diplomatic engagements led by President Eisenhower, Americans secured peace on the Korean Peninsula. On July 27, 1953, North Korea, China, and the United Nations signed an armistice suspending all hostilities. While the armistice stopped the active fighting in the region, North Korea's ballistic and nuclear weapons programs continue to pose grave threats to the United States and our allies and partners. At this moment, more than 28,000 American troops maintain a strong allied presence along the 38th parallel, which separates North and South Korea.

26 July 2017. Xinhua. Chinese President Xi Jinping has called for all-out efforts to push forward military reform with the support of the entire nation, and the Communist Party of China (CPC).

26 July 2017. Xinhua. All businesses operating within China need to properly register with the authorities, and every business with a website needs to obtain an Internet Content Provider license, and display it at the bottom on their website. Chinese law prohibits the spread of harmful, violent and terrorist information.

27 July 2017. The Russian President arrived in Savonlinna for talks with President of Finland Sauli Niinisto. The two presidents will discuss bilateral cooperation in trade and the economy, cultural and humanitarian areas, and environmental protection, and will exchange views on current regional and international issues. Mr. Putin and Mr. Niinisto will then visit Olavinlinna Castle, where an opera festival is taking place from July 7 to August 4. The two presidents will attend a performance of the opera Iolanta staged by

the Bolshoi Theatre.   Mr. Putin's visit is marking the 100th anniversary of Finland's independence as a state. After the official part of the visit was over, Vladimir Putin and Sauli Niinisto had a productive one-on-one discussion that lasted some 90 minutes.

28 July 2017. The White House. Statement from the President on North Korea's Second ICBM Launch.
North Korea's test launch today, 28 July, of another intercontinental ballistic missile—the second such test in less than a month—is only the latest reckless and dangerous action by the North Korean regime. The United States condemns this test and rejects the regime's claim that these tests—and these weapons—ensure North Korea's security. In reality, they have the opposite effect. By threatening the world, these weapons and tests further isolate North Korea, weaken its economy, and deprive its people. The United States will take all necessary steps to ensure the security of the American homeland and protect our allies in the region.

28 July 2017. The White House. President Donald J. Trump spoke today with King Abdullah II of Jordan to discuss the events that transpired in the region over the past two weeks.

28 July 2017. Russia has asked the U.S. to cut its embassy and other personnel in the country, and ousted it from properties in Moscow, retaliating against the passage late Thursday, 27 July, of a new sanctions bill in Congress.

30 July 2017. Xinhua. China needs to build strong armed forces more than any other time in history, as the Chinese nation is closer to the goal of great rejuvenation than ever, Xi said.
"The PLA has the confidence and capability to defeat all invading enemies, and safeguard China's national sovereignty, security and development interests," said Xi, also general secretary of the Communist Party of China (CPC) Central Committee and chairman of the Central Military Commission.
Xi, who was endorsed as the core of the CPC Central Committee in 2016, called on the PLA to stay loyal to the Party, boost combat capability, and continue to serve the people.

It is the first time for Xi to oversee such a large parade at a military base, and the first time for China to commemorate Army Day with a military parade, since the founding of the People's Republic of China in 1949. Today, the PLA commands about 2 millions of service personnel, one of the world's largest military forces.

Xi on Sunday, 30 July, again urged the PLA to focus on war preparedness, to forge an elite and powerful force that is always "ready for the fight, capable of combat, and sure to win."

Chinese servicemen are actively involved in international peace-keeping missions. The country has sent about 35,000 military personnel, the most among permanent members of the UN Security Council, to at least 24 UN peace-keeping missions.

China's crackdown on the internet is continuing with news that Apple was forced to remove all major VPN apps from its local App store, which help users overcome the country's "Great Firewall." Service providers criticized the move, calling it a "dangerous precedent."

China is speeding up underwater drone tests in the South China Sea.

China criticized the U.S. over North Korea, saying Washington was inflaming up tensions with Pyongyang, and violating U.N. Security Council resolutions, through its plan to impose unilateral sanctions.

Ageing with the help of technology is an important area of research and development, and medical robots play a key role.

New technologies and ever-faster computing speeds are enabling medical breakthroughs that can improve the health care.

An international team of scientists has developed a method to rapidly produce specific human antibodies in the laboratory.

Virginia Tech researchers have developed a new way to defrost surfaces, 10 times faster than normal.

Next-generation drones will fly and dive into the sea like pelicans.

New research from Stony Brook University reveals that sulfur dioxide, a major contributor to air pollution, is removed from the air by concrete surfaces

Canada, Niagara Falls: the American Falls (21-30 m drop, 290 m wide), the Bridal Veil Falls (right, 21m), after Luna Island

Chapter 8. August 2017

1 August 2017. The White House. Statement by President Donald J. Trump

The United States condemns the actions of the Maduro dictatorship. Mr. Lopez and Mr. Ledezma are political prisoners being held illegally by the regime. The United States holds Maduro – who publicly announced just hours earlier that he would move against his political opposition – personally responsible for the health and safety of Mr. Lopez, Mr. Ledezma, and any others seized. We reiterate our call for the immediate and unconditional release of all political prisoners.

1 August 2017. The U.S. has imposed sanctions against Venezuela's President Maduro, stating his government abused human rights and organized an illegitimate vote designed to advance an authoritarian regime.

Two of Venezuela's most prominent opposition leaders have been seized from their homes in what many called another alarming step toward President Maduro's autocratic rule.

2 August 2017. Chinese state media said President Trump is "wrong" when he says China can resolve the ongoing North Korea nuclear crisis on its own, emphasizing that it "doesn't have the kind of 'control' over Pyongyang that the U.S. president believes it does." "From Beijing's perspective, it has significantly increased the pressure on Pyongyang, by doing everything the strengthened UN sanctions regime requires of it."

3 August 2017. US Secretary of State Rex Tillerson said neither he nor President Donald Trump is "very happy" about new sanctions on Russia that Congress has voted to put in place. The remarks are in contrast with those of Vice President Mike Pence, who said the bill showed Trump and Congress are speaking "with a unified voice."

4 August 2017. The White House. President Donald J. Trump spoke today with President Emmanuel Macron of France to explore how to increase cooperation.

4 August 2017. After a month of deliberations and negotiations, the UN Security Council has unanimously passed a resolution that would slash $1B, or about a third, off North Korea's annual export revenue.

Since it went commercial roughly 20 years ago (1997), the internet has become a part of people's daily lives. Today's internet is a global network connecting more than 3.5 billions of users worldwide (about half of the world population) through 224 millions of websites. Every day, users send almost 270 millions of e-mails worldwide. The United States is the dominant force in all of this, but the cybercriminals are constantly attacking people on the internet.

4 August 2017. Xinhua. Chinese defense ministry has urged India to immediately pull back the trespassing troops to the Indian side of the boundary.

6 August 2017. The White House. President Donald J. Trump spoke today with President Moon Jae-in of South Korea to discuss North Korea's July 28 launch of an intercontinental ballistic missile. President Trump and President Moon welcomed the new United Nations Security Council resolution that unanimously passed 15-0.

China's cyber regulator is investigating the country's top social media sites over content banned by the Communist Party. The Cyberspace Administration said WeChat, Tieba and Weibo have users spreading "false rumors, and other hazards to national security, public safety and social order."

7 August 2017. Xinhua. China urges South Korea to stop further deployment of the U.S. Terminal High Altitude Area Defense (THAAD), and make efforts to improve their relations by removing the stumbling block between them, Chinese Foreign Minister Wang Yi said in Manila on Sunday, 6 August.

10 August 2017. Reports say that North Korea has responded back at threats from President Trump, branding his warnings "a load of nonsense" and stating only "absolute force can work on him." With the crisis taking place at its south border, China's foreign ministry has issued a statement calling on all relevant parties to avoid any words or action that could "intensify problems or escalate the situation." Chinese state press is saying that this is a game of chicken between the U.S. and North Korea, and that the two parties should get back to dialog.

11 August 2017. Venezuela's President Nicolas Maduro has called on President Trump to engage in a "personal conversation" just days after being hit with new U.S. sanctions for his creation of an all-powerful legislative assembly. "If he [Trump] is so interested in Venezuela, here I am," he said during a lengthy address. "Mr. Donald Trump, here is my hand."

11 August 2017. The White House. Today, Nicolas Maduro requested a phone call with President Donald J. Trump. Since the start of this Administration, President Trump has asked that Maduro respect Venezuela's constitution, hold free and fair elections, release political prisoners, cease all human rights violations, and stop oppressing Venezuela's great people. The Maduro regime has refused to heed this call, which has been echoed around the region and the world. Instead Maduro has chosen the path of dictatorship. The United States stands with the people of Venezuela in the face of their continued oppression by the Maduro regime. President Trump will gladly speak with the leader of Venezuela as soon as democracy is restored in that country.

Reports: President Trump warned of a "military option" before the weekend, on 11 August, telling reporters at his Bedminster, N.J., golf resort that it was "certainly something we could pursue."

12 August 2017. The White House President Donald J. Trump spoke yesterday, 11 August, with President Xi Jinping of China. The leaders affirmed that the recent adoption of a new United Nations Security Council resolution regarding North Korea was an

important and necessary step toward achieving peace and stability on the Korean Peninsula.

12 August 2017. The White House. President Donald J. Trump spoke today with President Emmanuel Macron of France. They discussed the need to confront the increasingly dangerous situation associated with North Korea's destabilizing and escalatory behavior.

14 August 2017. Reports say that Chinese President Xi moved to calm growing tensions about North Korea over the weekend, telling President Trump in a phone call that all sides should maintain restraint, and avoid inflammatory comments. The conversation came shortly after Trump added to his recent tweets by saying that U.S. military options were "now fully in place, locked and loaded, should North Korea act unwisely."

14 August 2017. Vladimir Putin had a telephone conversation with President of the Republic of Kazakhstan, Nursultan Nazarbayev.

14 August 2017. At Iran's initiative, Vladimir Putin had a telephone conversation with President of the Islamic Republic of Iran, Hassan Rouhani. Mr. Putin congratulated Mr. Rouhani on his inauguration ceremony on August 5, and wished him success in his continued work as President of Iran.
The two presidents discussed bilateral cooperation results, including the state of progress in joint oil and gas, electricity, and transport projects, and examined a number of issues on the international agenda. Exchanging views on developments in Syria, both leaders underscored their commitment to continue coordinating joint efforts to facilitate settlement of this crisis.

14 August 2017. Vladimir Putin had a telephone conversation with President of the Republic of Kyrgyzstan, Almazbek Atambayev.

15 August 2017. The White House. President Donald J. Trump spoke yesterday with Prime Minister Narendra Modi of India

to congratulate the 1.2 billion citizens of India, who will celebrate 70 years of freedom and independence on August 15.

15 August 2017. The White House President Donald J. Trump spoke today with Prime Minister Shinzo Abe of Japan. The two leaders exchanged views on the growing threat from the Democratic People's Republic of Korea (DPRK), including the DPRK's most recent threats to United States and Japanese territory.

15 August 2017. Xinhua. China and Pakistan on Sunday, 13 August, promised to deepen their pragmatic cooperation in various fields, during a meeting between Pakistani Prime Minister Shahid Khaqan Abbasi (58), and visiting Chinese Vice Premier Wang Yang (62).

15 August 2017. Reports say that Venezuela's armed forces are starting preparations for military exercises later this month, after President Trump warned of possible military action. "Venezuela will not be threatened," President Maduro declared, adding that Trump "should know that threatening Venezuela is like threatening Latin America." The warning from President Trump was rejected by the whole region, even countries opposed to Venezuela.

17 Aug 2017. Xinhua. Chinese border troops have always patrolled the Chinese side of the line of control on the China-India border, said a Foreign Ministry (FM) representative Wednesday, 16 Aug, in response to a recent altercation between the two troops.
According to media reports, Chinese and Indian soldiers yelled and threw stones at each other in Ladakh, a disputed area between China, Pakistan and India in southeastern Kashmir on Tuesday, 15 Aug.
The FM also urged India to immediately and unconditionally withdraw all troops and equipment that have encroached into Chinese territory in the Dong Lang (Doklam) area.
"This is the foundation and prerequisite to the solution of the incident". On June 18, more than 270 Indian border troops, carrying weapons and driving two bulldozers, crossed the boundary in the Sikkim Sector and advanced more than 100 meters into Chinese territory, to obstruct road construction by the Chinese side, causing tension in the area. The trespassing Indian troops numbered as many

as 400 people at one point. As of the end of July, there were still more than 40 Indian border troops and one bulldozer illegally remaining in the Chinese territory.

17 Aug 2017. China has reclaimed its position as the largest foreign holder of U.S. debt, displacing Japan which had held the top spot since October 2016. It has increased its holdings for the fifth straight month, buying $44.3 B of Treasuries in June for a total of $1.147 T. China and Japan account for more than a third of the total foreign ownership of U.S. Treasuries.

17 Aug 2017. Xinhua. China firmly opposes a U.S. report that made unreasonable assertions on religious freedom in China, a Foreign Ministry (FM) representative said in Beijing Wednesday, 16 Aug.
Media reported the United States on Tuesday, 15 Aug, issued its annual religious freedom report, calling out seven countries, including China, for serious problems in terms of religious freedom.

18 Aug 2017. The White House. President Donald J. Trump spoke today with President Mariano Rajoy of Spain, to extend his condolences to the victims and families of the August 17 terrorist attacks in Barcelona and Cambrils. President Trump pledged the full support of the United States in investigating the attack, and bringing the perpetrators and their associates to justice.

18 August 2017, Xinhua. Chinese President Xi Jinping on Thursday, 17 Aug, said he expects military relations would become a major stabilizing factor in Sino-U.S. ties.
Xi was meeting with Chairman of the U.S. Joint Chiefs of Staff Joseph Dunford at the Great Hall of the People in Beijing, the first senior military official to visit China since U.S. President Donald Trump took office.
During his visit, Dunford also met with Fang Fenghui, chief of the CMC Joint Staff Department; Fan Changlong, CMC vice chairman, and Chinese State Councilor Yang Jiechi.

18 Aug 2017. Reports say that President Macron was at 64% approval in June. Now, less than two months later, he has fallen to 36%.

18 Aug 2017. Xinhua. A Chinese Foreign Ministry (FM) representative said Friday, 18 Aug, that the Japanese ambassador to India should not wave his tongue too freely on the standoff between China and India in the Dong Lang (Doklam) area.
The representative told a routine press briefing that there is no territorial dispute in that area, and that the nature of the incident is that Indian troops illegally crossed the already delimited Sikkim section of the China-India boundary, into Chinese territory.
Japanese Ambassador to India Kenji Hiramatsu said in an interview with Indian media that Doklam is disputed territory between China and Bhutan, and no country should use force to change its status.
It is better not to make irresponsible remarks before making clear the facts, the FM said, stressing that it is India, not China, which is trying to create trouble, and change the status quo.

21 Aug 2017. Vladimir Putin issued an Executive Order appointing Anatoly Antonov (62, general) Ambassador Extraordinary and Plenipotentiary of the Russian Federation to the United States of America, and, concurrently, Permanent Observer of the Russian Federation at the Organization of American States in Washington, USA.

21 Aug 2017. China has responded to Friday's (18 Aug) announcement of a U.S. investigation into China's alleged theft of U.S. intellectual property, expressing "strong dissatisfaction" with the "unilateral, protectionist action." The Commerce Ministry will also adopt "all appropriate measures to resolutely defend China's interests."

21 Aug 2017. The upcoming U.S.-South Korea military exercises are "reckless behavior driving the situation into the uncontrollable phase of a nuclear war," warned North Korea, ahead of the 10-day event, which will include around 17,500 U.S. service members. Pyongyang followed last year's drills by launching missiles, and carrying out its fifth nuclear test.

22 Aug 2017. Vladimir Putin had a telephone conversation with Chancellor of the Federal Republic of Germany Angela Merkel, President of the French Republic Emmanuel Macron and President of Ukraine Petro Poroshenko.

The telephone conversation with Angela Merkel, Emmanuel Macron, and Petro Poroshenko resulted in the following joint statement: "On August 22, 2017, the heads of state and government of the Normandy Format countries – Russia, Germany, France and Ukraine – had a telephone conversation.

The leaders voiced their firm support for the decision the Contact Group is expected to make on August 23 to declare a ceasefire in connection with the start of a new school year.

The leaders expressed hope that the ceasefire would lead to a stable improvement of the security situation for the benefit of schoolchildren, and the entire civilian population of Donbass.

On the basis of a stable ceasefire the leaders undertook to continue providing personal assistance to the further implementation of the Package of Measures adopted in Minsk in February 2015."

23 Aug 2017. Vladimir Putin met in Sochi with Prime Minister of Israel, Benjamin Netanyahu, who is in Russia on a short working visit. Mr. Putin and Mr. Netanyahu exchanged views on developing bilateral relations, and on the situation in the Middle East.

23 Aug 2017. Vladimir Putin met with President of Armenia, Serzh Sargsyan (63), in Sochi, Russia.

23 August 2017. Vladimir Putin received Secretary of State of the Vatican, Cardinal Pietro Parolin, at his Sochi residence.
On the agenda were key matters in relations between Russia and the Vatican in political, cultural and humanitarian areas.

23 August 2017. Reports say that the American government has placed new sanctions on Chinese and Russian firms and individuals, which have traded oil and other mineral resources with North Korea Kim Jong-un's regime.

23 Aug 2017. Due to its failure to make progress on respecting human rights and democratic norms, the U.S. has decided to deny Egypt $95.7 M in aid, and delay a further $195 M, CNBC reports. American officials were especially unhappy that President Sisi allowed a new law governing NGOs to go into effect, which is widely seen as part of a growing crackdown on dissent.

24 Aug 2017. Reports say that Qatar has restored diplomatic relations with Iran, in a move set to further increase tensions with the four Arab states it has been in a regional dispute with, since June. Qatar and other Gulf states withdrew their ambassadors to Iran in early 2016, after mobs damaged Saudi diplomatic facilities in the country, following the execution of a Shia cleric in Saudi Arabia.

25 Aug 2017. Xinhua. President Xi Jinping said on Thursday, 24 Aug, that he is ready to make concerted efforts with President Moon Jae-in of the Republic of Korea, to properly address the differences between the two countries.
Xi made the remark as he and Moon exchanged congratulatory messages on the 25th anniversary of the establishment of diplomatic relations between the two nations.
Seoul's ties with Beijing have been frustrated the past year over the deployment of the US Terminal High-Altitude Area Defense antimissile system in the ROK.

25 Aug 2017. The White House. The Maduro dictatorship continues to deprive the Venezuelan people of food and medicine, imprison the democratically-elected opposition, and violently suppress freedom of speech.

28 Aug 2017. The White House. On Monday, 28 Aug, President Trump welcomed President Niinistö of Finland to the White House for a bilateral meeting.

28 Aug 2017. The White House. President Donald J. Trump spoke on Thursday, 24 Aug, with President Abdel Fattah Al Sisi of Egypt to underscore the importance of the United States-Egypt relationship.

28 Aug 2017. The Russian President arrived in Budapest at the invitation of Prime Minister of Hungary, Viktor Orban.

Mr. Putin's visit coincides with the opening ceremony of the 2017 World Judo Championships, which is taking place in Budapest. The President of Russia is honorary president of the International Judo Federation. As part of his visit to Hungary, Vladimir Putin met with President of Mongolia, Khaltmaagiin Battulga.

28 Aug 2017. Reports say that North Korea fired several ballistic missiles off its east coast on Saturday, 26 Aug, which flew for about 250 km, as the South and U.S. conducted their annual joint military drills.

28 Aug 2017. Reports say that India and China have agreed to an "expeditious disengagement" of troops in the disputed Doklam region, where their soldiers have been locked in a stand-off since June. The decision comes ahead of next week's summit of BRICS nations - a grouping that also includes Brazil, Russia and South Africa. The bloc has created a $100 B development bank and a $100 B emergency fund.

29 Aug 2017. Reports say that North Korea fired a ballistic missile over Japan, while the U.S. and South Korea wrapped up their annual military drills in the area. Describing the test as an "unprecedented, grave threat," Prime Minister Shinzo Abe called for an emergency meeting of the UN Security Council.

29 Aug 2017. The White House. President Donald J. Trump spoke yesterday, 28 Aug, with Prime Minister Shinzo Abe of Japan, to address North Korea's launch of a missile that overflew Japanese territory. The two leaders agreed that North Korea poses a grave and growing direct threat to the United States, Japan, and the Republic of Korea, as well as to countries around the world.

29 Aug 2017. The White House. President Donald J. Trump spoke on the phone today with Prime Minister Lee Hsien Loong of Singapore, to discuss hurricane response efforts.

29 Aug 2017. Mexican President Enrique Pena Nieto is scheduled to hold a bilateral meeting with China's President Xi Jinping at the BRICS summit next week, as it looks to decrease its dependence on NAFTA. He'll also visit the offices of Alibaba. It comes as Mexico takes part in three days of talks in Australia, aimed at reviving the Trans-Pacific Partnership trade agreement.

29 August 2017. The dispute between Catalonia and the central government of Spain has escalated in recent days. Pro-separatist parties are going ahead with legal preparations to create an independent state, as they prepare for a disputed referendum on secession in October. The region's previous non-binding poll in 2014, which was ruled illegal by Madrid, saw 80% in favor of full secession.

29 Aug 2017. Xinhua. China on Monday, 28 Aug, confirmed via on-site checks, that India has withdrawn personnel and equipment from Dong Lang (Doklam), after a military stand-off lasting more than two months.

30 Aug 2017. The White House. President Donald J. Trump spoke today by telephone with Prime Minister Shinzo Abe of Japan. The two leaders confirmed their continuing, close cooperation on efforts to address North Korea's launch of an intermediate range ballistic missile that overflew Japanese territory earlier this week.

30 Aug 2017. The White House. President Donald J. Trump spoke today with King Salman bin Abdulaziz Al Saud of Saudi Arabia.

30 Aug 2017. Reports say that one of the episodes of ISIS's occupation in the Middle East has drawn to a close, with Lebanon reclaiming all the land that the terrorist group had controlled in the country for the past three years. Moody's lifted the country's outlook to stable from negative, in response.

30 Aug 2017. Xinhua. Yang Liwei, deputy director of China Manned Space Engineering Office, has gone on-record saying that

China welcomes more countries to participate in the construction and operation of its new manned space station.

The suggestion comes after a group of 16 astronauts, including Yang Liwei and Jing Haipeng, as well as two European astronauts, completed sea survival training in the ocean off the coast of Yantai, Shandong Province, on August 21, 2017.

31 Aug 2017. The White House. President Donald J. Trump today spoke with Prime Minister Justin Trudeau of Canada, to address the continuing devastation from catastrophic flooding in Texas and Louisiana caused by a hurricane.

31 Aug 2017. Reports say that President Trump tweeted on Wednesday (30 Aug 2017): "The U.S. has been talking to North Korea, and paying them extortion money, for 25 years. Talking is not the answer!" Defense Secretary James Mattis said the U.S. is "never out of diplomatic solutions." Secretary of State Rex Tillerson also expressed hopes last week that the U.S. would be open to "some dialogue" with North Korea.

31 Aug 2017. Xinhua. Chinese President Xi Jinping viewed an honor guard, with visiting President of Tajikistan, Emomali Rahmon (65), during a welcome ceremony before their talks in Beijing, capital of China. Rahmon is paying a state visit to China. During his stay in China, he will attend the Dialogue of Emerging Markets and Developing Countries held in Xiamen, a coastal city in southeast China's Fujian Province

Chinese President Xi Jinping held talks with President of Tajikistan Emomali Rahmon on Thursday, 31 Aug, agreeing to establish comprehensive strategic partnership between the two countries.

University of California, Irvine, scientists, studying how aging affects the biological clock's control of metabolism, have discovered that a low-calorie diet helps keep these energy-regulating processes humming, and the body younger.

Americans had a spectacular total Solar eclipse on August 21 in an approximately 112 km-wide zone stretching from the Northwest (Oregon) to the Southeast.(South Carolina) In New

Jersey, a partial eclipse started at about 1:20 PM., and peaked at about 2:45 PM.

Australia, Sydney. From College Street, looking east to the west main entrance of St. Mary's Cathedral (1821, 1865, 1928, 75 m height, built of local sandstone and granite, Roman Catholic Archdiocese of Sydney).

Chapter 9. September 2017

1 Sep 2017. The White House. President Donald J. Trump spoke today with President Moon Jae-in of South Korea to discuss our coordinated response to North Korea's continued destabilizing and escalatory behavior. President Trump provided his conceptual approval of planned purchases by South Korea of billions of dollars in American military equipment.

1 Sep 2017. The White House. President Donald J. Trump today spoke with President Juan Manuel Santos of Colombia, who expressed solidarity with the United States and offered the support and sympathy of the Colombian people to hurricane survivors. President Trump stressed the importance of Colombia doing its utmost to eliminate the production and trafficking of illegal drugs.

1 Sep 2017. The White House. President Donald J. Trump spoke today with President Nursultan Nazarbayev of Kazakhstan to discuss the two countries' 25-year relationship.

1 Sep 2017. Reports say that Russia Foreign Minister Sergey Lavrov (67) declared that Russia has yet to study the U.S. decision to shut its consulate in San Francisco and annexes in New York and Washington, DC, before considering possible retaliation. The Trump administration just gave Russia 72 hours yesterday (31 Aug) to close three of its diplomatic facilities in America, in retaliation for asking more than 700 U.S. diplomats, last month, to leave Russia. Russian President Vladimir Putin in July ordered the U.S. to reduce the number of diplomatic personnel in Russia by 755, in response to U.S. sanctions on Russia.

Earlier, U.S. President Donald Trump said that he hoped the U.S. could have good relations with Russia, which would be "good for world peace." "I hope that we do have good relations with Russia," Trump said at a joint press conference with visiting Finnish President Sauli Niinisto. "I say it loud and clear. I have been saying it for years. I think it's a good thing if we have great relationships, or at least good relationships, with Russia."

"I believe someday that will happen...I think that's very good for world peace and other things," the U.S. President added.

1 Sep 2017. Xinhua. Kenya's Supreme Court on Friday (1 Sep) declared the Aug. 8 presidential election null and void, and ordered a repeat of similar exercise within 60 days.

2 Sep 2017. The White House. President Donald J. Trump spoke today with Prime Minister Shinzo Abe of Japan to discuss ongoing efforts to maximize pressure on North Korea.

2 Sep 2017. Xinhua. Chinese President Xi Jinping and his Brazilian counterpart Michel Temer on Friday (1 Sep) agreed to further advance the comprehensive strategic partnership between the two countries. Temer is in China for a state visit at the invitation of Xi. During his stay, Temer will also attend the BRICS summit, and the Dialogue of Emerging Markets and Developing Countries, to be held in China's southeastern coastal city of Xiamen, in Fujian Province from Sept. 3 to 5.

2 Sep 2017. Xinhua. U.S. Defense Secretary James Mattis said Thursday (31 Aug) that he has signed orders to send additional troops to Afghanistan.
Mattis told reporters at the Pentagon that he will not reveal details until he briefs Congress next week. However, he said that the additional troops will include advisers and support personnel that will enable the Afghan force to fight more effectively.
U.S. media have reported that about 4,000 more troops will be deployed in Afghanistan. The move came after U.S. President Donald Trump unveiled his new Afghanistan strategy Monday (28 Aug) night in a national address, calling a rapid exit of the U.S. troops from Afghanistan "unacceptable", and pledging a shift from a time-based approach to one based on conditions.
On Wednesday (30 Aug), Pentagon representative said that 11,000 U.S. troops are currently in Afghanistan, thousands more than the previously acknowledged 8,400. The 8,400 number did not include troops on temporary assignment, according to the Pentagon.

3 Sep 2017. North Korea (DPRK)'s official media announced on Sunday (3 Sep) that the country has successfully detonated a hydrogen bomb, capable of being carried by an intercontinental ballistic missile (ICBM).

UN Secretary-General Antonio Guterres Sunday (3 Sep) condemned the underground nuclear test announced by the Democratic People's Republic of Korea (DPRK).

Chinese Foreign Ministry issued a statement on Sunday, 3 Sep, expressing firm opposition to, and strong condemnation of the nuclear test by the DPRK. "The DPRK has ignored the international community's widespread opposition, and conducted a nuclear test again. The Chinese government expresses resolute objection to, and strong condemnation of it," the ministry's statement said.

3 Sep 2017. The White House. President Donald J. Trump spoke with Prime Minister Shinzo Abe of Japan to discuss North Korea's claimed test of a hydrogen bomb, on September 3.

3 Sep 2017. Vladimir Putin had talks with President of the People's Republic of China, Xi Jinping, in Xiamen, China.
The two leaders discussed, in particular, current issues of Russia-China cooperation, including the implementation of bilateral agreements, as well as a number of international issues.
The talks were held ahead of the Russian President's participation in the BRICS Summit and the meeting of the BRICS Business Council.
On the sidelines of the summit, Vladimir Putin will also meet with Prime Minister of India Narendra Modi, President of the South African Republic Jacob Zuma (75) and invited guests, Egyptian President Abdel Fattah el-Sisi, Prime Minister of Thailand Prayut Chan-o-cha (63), and President of Mexico, Enrique Peña Nieto .
The Russian President's visit to China will last until September 5.
President XI: "This time, we chose Xiamen purposefully – Xiamen University, with its nearly 100-year history, is located in close proximity. The university has a monument to Russian poet Mikhail Lermontov (1814-1841, aged 26, second greatest Russian poet after Alexander Pushkin (1799-1837, aged 37)). Interestingly, the monument is located just opposite the monument to the great Chinese philosopher Confucius (551 BC – 479 BC, aged 72). It is

obvious that people in this city value the cultural exchange between China and Russia. I know a famous poem by Lermontov called "The Sail," which praises a persistent struggle and a strong will."

While discussing international and regional issues, the two leaders agreed to appropriately deal with the DPRK's latest nuclear test.

The DPRK on Sunday (3 Sep) successfully detonated a hydrogen bomb that can be carried by an intercontinental ballistic missile (ICBM), DPRK's Central Television announced. This was the sixth nuclear test the DPRK has undertaken.

China's Foreign Ministry issued a statement, expressing firm opposition to, and strong condemnation of the nuclear test.

Xi and Putin agreed to stick to the goal of denuclearization on the Korean Peninsula, and keep close communication and coordination to deal with the new situation.

3 Sep 2017. During his visit to Xiamen, China, in connection with the BRICS summit, Vladimir Putin had a telephone conversation with Prime Minister of Japan Shinzo Abe.

The two leaders had a substantial exchange of opinions on the aggravated situation on the Korean Peninsula, condemning the nuclear test conducted by the Democratic People's Republic of Korea on September 3, 2017, as it undermines the global non-proliferation regime, violates UN Security Council resolutions and norms of international law, and poses a real threat to regional peace and stability. Vladimir Putin said the international community should not give way to emotions, but rather to keep its composure and act reasonably, and he also emphasized that a comprehensive solution, to the nuclear and other issues on the Korean peninsula, can be reached through political and diplomatic methods only.

Vladimir Putin and Shinzo Abe agreed to continue their dialogue on the issue during the Eastern Economic Forum in Vladivostok, Russia, on September 7.

3 Sep 2017. Vladimir Putin took part in a meeting of the BRICS leaders that was held within the framework of the two-day BRICS summit in Xiamen, China.

President of Russia Vladimir Putin, President of China Xi Jinping, President of Brazil Michel Temer, Prime Minister of India Narendra

Modi, and President of South Africa Jacob Zuma met in a restricted format, before their delegations joined the consultations.

4 Sep 2017. The White House. President Donald J. Trump spoke today with President Moon Jae-in of South Korea, to discuss the allied response to North Korea's claimed September 3 test of a hydrogen bomb.

4 Sep 2017. The White House. President Donald J. Trump spoke today with Chancellor Angela Merkel of Germany to discuss North Korea's claimed September 3 test of a hydrogen bomb.

4 Sep 2017. Vladimir Putin held a meeting with Indian Prime Minister Narendra Modi on the sidelines of the BRICS summit in Xiamen. Current topics and prospects for the development of relations between the two countries were discussed.

4 Sep 2017. Xinhua. Chinese President Xi Jinping said Monday (4 Sep) China and Mexico should synergize development strategies on the basis of their cooperative achievements since the two sides forged diplomatic ties 45 years ago.
Xi made the remarks when meeting with Mexican President Enrique Pena Nieto, who came to the southeastern Chinese coastal city of Xiamen, to attend the Dialogue of Emerging Market and Developing Countries, scheduled for Sept. 5.

4 Sep 2017. Vladimir Putin had a telephone conversation, from Xiamen, China, with President of the Republic of Korea, Moon Jae-in. Discussing the situation on the Korean Peninsula, following the nuclear test carried out by the DPRK on September 3, the two presidents firmly condemned Pyongyang's actions, which are in flagrant violation of the corresponding UN Security Council resolutions, undermining the global non-proliferation regime, and creating a serious threat to peace and security in the region.
Mr. Putin stressed that this extremely complex situation can be resolved exclusively through a renewal of negotiations, and the active use of political and diplomatic measures.

The two presidents will continue their exchange of views on this matter during their meeting on September 6, at the Eastern Economic Forum in Vladivostok, Russia.

4 Sep 2017. Xinhua. Chinese President Xi Jinping met with Thai Prime Minister Prayut Chan-o-cha on Monday (4 Sep), calling for enhanced bilateral cooperation in various fields.
Prayut is in the southeastern Chinese coastal city of Xiamen, to attend the Dialogue of Emerging Market and Developing Countries scheduled for Sept. 5.

4 Sep 2017. Vladimir Putin met in Xiamen, China, with President of the Arab Republic of Egypt, Abdel Fattah el-Sisi, to discuss development of bilateral cooperation in various areas.

4 Sep 2017. Vladimir Putin had a meeting with President of the Republic of South Africa, Jacob Zuma, on the sidelines of the BRICS summit in Xiamen, China.

5 Sep 2017. Vladimir Putin met with President of the United Mexican States, Enrique Pena Nieto.
The two presidents discussed the current state and future of bilateral trade, economic, investment, and energy relations, as well as opportunities for stepping up humanitarian contact and cooperating on foreign policy matters, including within various international organizations and on pressing regional issues.

5 Sep 2017. Vladimir Putin has met with the Prime Minister of the Kingdom of Thailand, Prayuth Chan-o-cha.
The discussion covered various aspects of bilateral cooperation, in particular, the prospects for increasing trade and economic contacts and the development of humanitarian ties.

5 Sep 2017. Vladimir Putin attended a meeting of BRICS leaders with delegation heads from invited states, including the heads of state and government of Egypt, Tajikistan, Mexico, Guinea and Thailand.

5 Sep 2017. Russian Defense Minister Sergei Shoigu (62) reported to the Commander-in-Chief Putin, on the completion of the operation to lift the terrorists' siege of the Syrian town of Deir ez-Zor. The Russian Aerospace Forces, with the support of Navy ships stationed in the Mediterranean Sea, carried out missile strikes on terrorist strongholds outside the town of Deir ez-Zor.

The air strikes caused damage to the infrastructure, underground utility lines and ammunition stores of terrorists, which allowed the Syrian government troops to launch an offensive, and break the siege of the town.

Vladimir Putin noted the importance of this strategic victory in terms of liberating Syria from ISIS, and congratulated the command of the Russian military group, as well as the command of the Syrian government troops, on this accomplishment.

President Putin sent a message to President of the Syrian Arab Republic, Bashar al-Assad, in which he highly praised this strategic victory, and offered congratulations on this important step on the way to liberating Syria from terrorism.

6 Sep 2017. The White House. President Donald J. Trump spoke today with President Xi Jinping of China, to discuss North Korea's September 3 test of a powerful nuclear device.

6 Sep 2017. The White House. President Donald J. Trump spoke yesterday (5 Sep) with Prime Minister Theresa May of the United Kingdom, to discuss North Korea's claimed September 3 test of a hydrogen bomb.

6 Sep 2017. The White House. President Donald J. Trump spoke yesterday (5 Sep) with Prime Minister Malcolm Turnbull of Australia, to discuss North Korea's claimed test of a hydrogen bomb on September 3

6 Sep 2017. The White House. President Donald J. Trump spoke today with King Salman bin Abdulaziz Al Saud of Saudi Arabia.

6 Sep 2017. Xinhua. Chinese President Xi Jinping said Tuesday, 5 Sep, healthy and stable relations between China and India are in line with the fundamental interests of their people.

6 Sep 2017. Vladimir Putin had a meeting with Vice Premier of the People's Republic of China State Council, Wang Yang, in Vladivostok, Russia.

6 Sep 2017. Vladimir Putin held talks with President of the Republic of Korea, Moon Jae-in, in Vladivostok.
The two leaders discussed prospects for promoting bilateral relations, in particular trade and economic cooperation, as well as current regional issues. A package of documents has been signed during the South Korean President's visit to Russia, and his attendance of the Eastern Economic Forum
An intergovernmental agreement on the establishment of a direct encrypted communications link between Russia and the Republic of Korea has been signed.
The parties also signed a memorandum on the participation of the Republic of Korea as a partner country in the 9th International Industrial Trade Fair INNOPROM 2018, and memorandums of understanding and cooperation between Russian organizations and the Korea Trade-Investment Promotion Agency (KOTRA). The concerned agencies of the two countries have signed a memorandum of understanding on cooperation in innovations, and a protocol of intent on cooperation in professional medical education. The parties also signed documents on the implementation of the Russian-Korean initiative for financial cooperation in the development of the Far East, and on the creation of a fish processing and logistics complex in the Russian Far East. Several other documents on practical aspects of cooperation between various Russian and Korean organizations have also been signed.

7 Sep 2017. The White House. President Trump welcomed the Amir Sabah al-Ahmed al-Jaber al-Sabah of Kuwait (88).

7 Sep 2017. Vladimir Putin held talks with Japanese Prime Minister Shinzo Abe in Vladivostok, to discuss prospects for the development of bilateral relations, and current regional issues.

7 Sep 2017. Vladimir Putin met with President of Mongolia Khaltmaagiin Battulga on the sidelines of the Eastern Economic Forum in Vladivostok, to discuss the prospects for strengthening bilateral relations, and also current regional and international issues.

8 Sep 2017. The White House. President Donald J. Trump spoke separately today with Crown Prince Mohamed bin Salman Al Saud of Saudi Arabia, Crown Prince Mohammed bin Zayed Al Nahyan of the United Arab Emirates, and Amir Tameem bin Hamad Al Thani of Qatar.

8 Sep 2017. Reports say that French President Emmanuel Macron has vowed to lead a "rebuilding" of the EU, proposing a "new deal", according to which deficit countries will repair their finances, and overhaul their economies. "In order not to be ruled by bigger powers such as the Chinese and the Americans, I believe in an European sovereignty that allows us to defend ourselves and exist," he said during a visit to Greece.

8 Sep 2017. The White House. President Donald J. Trump spoke today with President Emmanuel Macron of France to extend his condolences for the devastation and loss of life on the French territories of St. Barthélemy and St. Martin, due to a hurricane. President Trump offered support to the French government during this tragic time.

8 Sep 2017. Xinhua. Chinese President Xi Jinping on Friday (8 Sep) held a telephone conversation with his French counterpart, Emmanuel Macron, on the Korean Peninsula issue, stressing China's insistence that the peninsula be denuclearized.

8 Sep 2017. The White House. President Donald J. Trump spoke yesterday, 7 Sep, with Amir Tamim bin Hamad Al Thani of Qatar.

8 Sep 2017. Xinhua. Chinese President Xi Jinping said Thursday (7 Sep) that the international community should make a concerted effort to solve the nuclear issue on the Korean Peninsula.

During a telephone conversation with German Chancellor Angela Merkel, Xi said facts have repeatedly proven that an ultimate settlement of the nuclear issue could only be found through peaceful means, including dialogue and consultation

9 Sep 2017. The White House. President Donald J. Trump spoke today with President Recep Tayyip Erdogan of Turkey. President Trump emphasized the common commitment of the United States and Turkey to work together to increase regional stability.

11 Sep 2017. The White House. The United States is deeply troubled by the ongoing crisis in northern Rakhine State in Burma (Myanmar), where at least 300,000 people have fled their homes in the wake of attacks on Burmese security posts on August 25. We reiterate our condemnation of those attacks and ensuing violence.

11 Sep 2017. At the initiative of the German side, Vladimir Putin had a telephone conversation with Federal Chancellor of the Federal Republic of Germany, Angela Merkel. Vladimir Putin and Angela Merkel exchanged views on the current situation on the Korean Peninsula, in the context of the latest provocative actions by the DPRK, and strongly condemned Pyongyang's disregard of UN Security Council resolutions. It was noted that such steps are contrary to the principles of global non-proliferation, and pose a serious threat to regional peace and security.
It was confirmed that this acute crisis can only be resolved by political and diplomatic means, by resuming negotiations of all the parties involved. It was agreed to continue discussing the situation at the level of the foreign ministers of the two countries.
The implementation of the Minsk agreements on the settlement in southeast Ukraine was addressed.

12 Sep 2017. The White House. President Donald J. Trump spoke today with Crown Prince Mohammed bin Zayed Al Nahyan of the United Arab Emirates, to discuss efforts to resolve the ongoing dispute with Qatar.

12 Sep 2017. Reports say that U.S. solders conducted sling load and air assault training with M777A2 howitzers, during Saber Strike 2017, at the Bemowo Piskie training area near Orzysz, Poland.

12 Sep 2017. The total value of the U.S. national debt has surpassed the $20 T mark for the first time in the history of the nation. The problem isn't likely to get better anytime soon; the 2017 fiscal year budget ends Sept. 30, and is slated to add another $700 B deficit. U.S. debt also exceeds GDP, which was estimated to be roughly $19.23 T

According to the USDA, about 44 M individuals benefit from food stamps in the U.S.

13 Sep 2017. The White House. The President of the United States of America, Donald J. Trump, hosted the Prime Minister of Malaysia, Najib Razak (64), at the White House to strengthen the Comprehensive Partnership between the two countries, as they mark the 60th anniversary of bilateral relations.

13 Sep 2017. The White House. The United States Government seriously considered designating Colombia as a country that has failed demonstrably to adhere to its obligations under international counternarcotics agreements, due to the extraordinary growth of coca cultivation and cocaine production over the past 3 years, including record cultivation during the last 12 months. Ultimately, Colombia is not designated, because the Colombian National Police and Armed Forces are close law enforcement and security partners of the United States in the Western Hemisphere, they are improving interdiction efforts, and have restarted some eradication that they had significantly curtailed beginning in 2013. The President will, however, keep this designation as an option, and expect Colombia to make significant progress in reducing coca cultivation and production of cocaine.

13 Sep 2017. The White House. The President designated Bolivia and Venezuela as countries that have failed demonstrably

during the previous 12 months to adhere to their obligations under international counternarcotics agreements.

13 Sep 2017. Vladimir Putin met, at his Bocharov Ruchei residence, with Prime Minister of Lebanon, Saad Hariri, to discuss prospects for developing bilateral relations, and the situation in the region.

13 Sep 2017. The White House. The United States Government support for programs to aid the people of Venezuela are vital to the national interests of the United States.

13 Sep 2017. Vladimir Putin met, at his Bocharov Ruchei residence in Sochi, with Special Envoy of the Iranian President, Iranian Foreign Minister, Mohammad Javad Zarif (57).
The discussion focused on the situation in the Middle East, particularly in Syria, Iraq, and the Persian Gulf region, and the fight against terrorism.

13 Sep 2017. The White House. The President identified the following countries as major drug transit, and/or major illicit drug producing countries: Afghanistan, The Bahamas, Belize, Bolivia, Burma, Colombia, Costa Rica, Dominican Republic, Ecuador, El Salvador, Guatemala, Haiti, Honduras, India, Jamaica, Laos, Mexico, Nicaragua, Pakistan, Panama, Peru, and Venezuela.

14 Sep 2017. Xinhua. Chinese President Xi Jinping held talks with Brunei's Sultan Haji Hassanal Bolkiah (71) in Beijing on Wednesday (13 Sep), with the two agreeing to promote cooperation within the Belt and Road Initiative, and work for stronger bilateral ties. "China appreciates Brunei's efforts in strengthening China-ASEAN relations, and hopes to align the Belt and Road Initiative with ASEAN's development plan," Xi said.

14 Sep 2017. Xinhua. The Sino-Russian comprehensive university alliance was established Wednesday (13 Sep) in the south China city of Shenzhen. Forty Chinese universities, including Beijing's Peking and Tsinghua universities, and 20 Russian universities, including Lomonosov Moscow State University, joined

19 Sep 2017. President Donald J. Trump addressed the entire body of foreign dignitaries at the 72nd Session of the United Nations General Assembly in New York City. He urged leaders to invest in the strength of their own countries and pursue policies that increase stability and prosperity for their citizens.

19 Sep 2017. The White House. Last night, President Donald J. Trump hosted a working dinner in New York with President Michel Temer of Brazil, President Juan Manuel Santos of Colombia, President Juan Carlos Varela of Panama, and Vice President Gabriela Michetti of Argentina.

19 Sep 2017. The White House. President Trump and Emir Tamim bin Hamad Al Thani of Qatar had a bilateral meeting in New York.

20 Sep 2017. The White House. President Trump and Prime Minister May of the United Kingdom had a bilateral meeting.

20 Sep 2017. The White House. President Donald J. Trump met today with His Majesty King Abdullah II of Jordan in New York.

20 Sep 2017. President Donald J. Trump spoke today with United Nations Secretary-General Antonio Guterres. President Trump pledged his support for the Secretary-General's efforts to reform the United Nations, focusing on three pillars: peace and security, development, and management reform.

20 Sep 2017. Xinhua. President Xi Jinping on Tuesday (19 Sep) stressed the importance of preventing and controlling major risks through the leadership of the Communist Party of China.

20 Sep 2017. The White House. President Trump and President Abbas of the Palestinian Authority had a bilateral meeting.

20 Sep 2017. Vladimir Putin expressed his condolences to President of the United Mexican States Enrique Pena Nieto over the

numerous casualties, and devastation caused by an earthquake in the country's southeast. Vladimir Putin emphasized that Russia is ready to provide the necessary assistance to friendly Mexico in overcoming the consequences of this natural disaster.

21 Sep 2017. The White House. President Trump and Prime Minister Abe of Japan had a bilateral meeting in New York.

21 Sep 2017. The White House. President Trump, President Moon of the Republic of Korea, and Prime Minister Abe of Japan had a trilateral meeting in New York.

21 Sep 2017. The White House. President Trump and President Ghani of Afghanistan had a bilateral meeting in New York.

21 Sep 2017. The White House. President Trump and President Moon of the Republic of Korea had a bilateral meeting in New York.

21 Sep 2017. The White House. President Trump and President Poroshenko of Ukraine had a bilateral meeting in New York.

21 Sep 2017. The White House. President Trump and President Erdoğan of Turkey had a bilateral meeting in New York.

21 Sep 2017. The White House. President Donald J. Trump met with President Abdel Fattah Al Sisi of Egypt in New York.

22 Sep 2017. Reports say that a mild sell-off in China, which is the largest exporter, followed a downgrade of the country's sovereign credit by Standard & Poor's.

25 Sep 2017. The White House. President Donald J. Trump announced enhanced national security measures, and new requirements. Countries that do not adequately adhere to the new requirements include Chad, Iran, Libya, North Korea, Syria, Venezuela, and Yemen.

25 Sep 2017. Xinhua. Chinese President Xi Jinping on Monday (25 Sep) held a phone conversation with British Prime Minister Theresa May, on bilateral ties, and the situation on the Korean Peninsula. A prosperous, stable and open Britain and European Union conform to the interests of all parties, Xi told May, adding that China is willing to promote further development of China-Britain and China-EU relations.

Xi also said the Korean Peninsula issue should be solved through peaceful means, including dialogue and consultation, which needs joint efforts by the international community.

25 Sep 2017. Xinhua. Chinese President Xi Jinping has encouraged eight students from Nankai University, who joined the army this year, to help the country achieve its goal of building a strong army.

25 Sep 2017. Vladimir Putin had a telephone conversation with President of Kazakhstan, Nursultan Nazarbayev.

The two leaders discussed further prospects for the Syrian peace process, as they pertain to the results of the 6th international meeting on Syria, which took place in Astana on September 14–15. They stated that the Astana format has proved its efficiency, and contributes to easing tensions, and improving the humanitarian situation in Syria.

25 Sep 2017. Xinhua. South Korea's presidential Blue House said Monday (25 Sep) that the country had consulted with the United States in advance on the flight of U.S. strategic bombers and fighter escorts, in the international airspace, last weekend near the Democratic People's Republic of Korea (DPRK).

A Blue House official told local reporters that President Moon Jae-in was briefed on consultations on the flights, on a real-time basis, during his stay in New York last week, saying the close consultation between South Korea and the United States was reported to President Moon.

B-1B strategic bombers from the U.S. Pacific island of Guam, and F-15C fighter escorts from Okinawa, Japan, flew in the international airspace over the waters, off the east coast of the DPRK, Saturday (23 Sep) night, according to media reports.

It was an apparent show of force to the DPRK, as the war of words was resumed between Pyongyang and Washington, after U.S. President Donald Trump said, in his debut speech to the United Nations, that his country would have no choice but to "totally destroy" the DPRK, if Pyongyang continues to threaten the United States and its allies.

25 Sep 2017. Vladimir Putin had a telephone conversation with President of Turkey, Recep Tayyip Erdogan, at the Russian side's initiative. The two presidents discussed the Syrian issue, including the positive results of the 6th International Meeting on Syria held in Astana on September 14–15. It was stressed that the establishment of four de-escalation zones in the Syrian Arab Republic has opened a path toward ending the civil war, and a political settlement of the crisis, based on the principles of the country's sovereignty and territorial integrity.

The parties noted the importance of further close coordination of Russia's and Turkey's efforts in matters related to Syria.

25 Sep 2017. Reports say that China is calling on Pyongyang and Washington to calm their rhetoric, after the latest war of words. North Korea's Foreign Minister Ri Yong Ho (74) told the UN General Assembly on Saturday (23 Sep) that targeting the U.S. mainland with its rockets was inevitable, after the "Mr. Evil President" called Kim Jong-un a "rocket man" on a suicide mission. In response, Trump warned "they won't be around much longer!"

25 Sep 2017. Vladimir Putin had a telephone conversation with President of the Islamic Republic of Iran, Hassan Rouhani.

In discussing the current situation in Syria, the two leaders highly praised the results of the 6th International Meeting on Syria in Astana on September 14–15, 2017, primarily in terms of establishing four de-escalation zones. Both sides expressed readiness for further joint efforts in the interests of achieving a long-term settlement of the Syrian crisis, in particular by strengthening cooperation between the guarantor countries of the Astana process, and promoting political negotiations under the auspices of the UN in Geneva.

26 Sep 2017. The White House. President Trump and President Rajoy of Spain had a bilateral meeting.

26 Sep 2017. Xinhua. China hopes to work closely with countries and international organizations on global security, and jointly build universal security for humankind, Chinese President Xi Jinping said in Beijing, Tuesday, 26 Sep.

Xi made the remarks in Beijing while addressing the opening ceremony of the 86th Interpol General Assembly.

26 Sep 2017. Vladimir Putin congratulated Federal Chancellor of Germany Angela Merkel on CDU/CSU's success in the September 24 Bundestag election. The two sides reaffirmed their readiness to carry on with business-like, mutually beneficial cooperation between Russia and the Federal Republic of Germany.

26 Sep 2017. Reports say that tensions between the U.S. and North Korea have reached a new level, as the country's foreign minister said President Trump's recent comments amount to a declaration of war, threatening to shoot down American warplanes outside North Korean airspace. The White House called the claim of a war declaration "absurd."

26 Sep 2017. Xinhua. The United States has not declared war on the Democratic People's Republic of Korea (DPRK), the White House said on Monday, 25 Sep, in response to remarks of the DPRK's top diplomat.

"Last weekend, Trump claimed that our leadership wouldn't be around much longer. He declared a war on our country," Ri Yong-ho, the DPRK foreign minister, told reporters earlier in New York.

"The whole world should clearly remember it was the U.S. who first declared war on our country," Ri said, referring to Trump's tweet message on Saturday, 23 Sep. In response, the White House denied that the United States had declared war on Pyongyang.

"We have not declared war on North Korea, and frankly the suggestion of that is absurd," White House representative told a regular briefing in Washington.

"Our goal is still the same. We continue to seek the peaceful denuclearization of the Korean Peninsula".

The DPRK foreign minister also said that the DPRK reserved the right to take countermeasures, including shooting down U.S. bombers even if they are not in its air space.

"Since the United States declared war on our country, we will have every right to take countermeasures, including the right to shoot down U.S. strategic bombers, even when they are not inside the airspace border of our country," Ri said.

On Saturday, 23 Sep, U.S. Air Force B-1B Lancer bombers and F-15C Eagle fighter escorts flew in international airspace over waters east of the DPRK, the Pentagon said.

"This is the farthest north of the Demilitarized Zone (DMZ) any U.S. fighter or bomber aircraft have flown" off the DPRK's coast in the 21st century, said the Pentagon, adding that the move underscored "the seriousness with which we take DPRK's reckless behavior."

U.S. President Donald Trump also talked tough on the DPRK. In his first speech at the UN General Assembly on Sept. 19, Trump threatened that the United States "will have no choice than to totally destroy" the country unless Pyongyang refrains from its nuclear tests and missile launches. Two days later, Trump also signed a new order to ramp up sanctions on the DPRK.

In response, DPRK's top leader Kim Jong Un vowed to retaliate, saying Trump "will face results beyond his expectation."

In a statement released on Friday, 22 Sep, Kim said "I am now thinking hard about what response he could have expected when he allowed such eccentric words to trip off his tongue," according to the official Korean Central News Agency. Kim also accused Trump of uttering "unprecedented rude nonsense that one has never heard from any of his predecessors," saying the threat to "totally destroy" a sovereign state has gone beyond the limit.

27 Sep 2017. Xinhua. Chinese President Xi Jinping has asked writers and artists across the country to focus on the people, and keep producing excellent works. Xi, also general secretary of

the Communist Party of China Central Committee, made the remarks in a written instruction on cultural and ideological progress.

27 Sep 2017. Russian President Vladimir Putin met with President of the Republic of Guinea and Chairperson of the African Union, Alpha Conde (79), who has come to Russia on an official visit at the invitation of the Russian President.

27 Sep 2017. Chemical disarmament completed in Russia. The President listened to a report via videoconference on the destruction of Russia's last remaining chemical weapons.

27 Sep 2017. Reports say that because of concerns about agricultural research spending, and government policy trends, the U.S. for the first time has dropped from the top spot in a global ranking of how well countries can feed their own people. Ireland is now the most "food-secure" nation, improving its affordability, availability and quality, according to the sixth annual Global Food Security Index.

28 Sep 2017. Reports say that Prime Minister May has threatened a trade war with the U.S., after the U.S. imposed punitive tariffs on Bombardier's British-built aircraft. May also warned that Boeing's long-term partnership with the government is being "undermined by this behavior." May has appealed directly to President Trump to intervene in the dispute, which has dented U.K. hopes of signing a post-Brexit free trade deal with the U.S.

28 Sep 2017. Ankara hosted talks between Vladimir Putin and President of the Republic of Turkey, Recep Tayyip Erdogan. President of Russia Vladimir Putin and President of Turkey Recep Tayyip Erdogan had a one-on-one conversation, after which Russian-Turkish talks continued in an expanded format.

28 Sep 2017. Reports say that Venezuela's President Maduro has called on his nation's military leaders to prepare for war against the U.S., stating "the future of humanity cannot be the world of illegal sanctions, of economic persecution." "We need to have rifles, missiles, and well-oiled tanks at the ready," he declared, after

President Trump said last month he wouldn't rule out a military option in the country.

29 Sep 2017. Xinhua. Chinese President Xi Jinping, also general secretary of the Communist Party of China (CPC) Central Committee, has called for a profound understanding of Marxism, and vigorous promotion of the sinicization of Marxism.
Xi made the remarks Friday, 29 Sep, afternoon at a group study session attended by members of the Political Bureau of the CPC Central Committee.

29 Sep 2017. Reports say that, according to the IAEA, North Korea's sixth nuclear test conducted on Sept. 3 showed the isolated country has made "rapid progress" on weapons development, and poses a "new threat." The warning comes after China, Pyongyang's most important ally, ordered North Korean companies in the country, and joint ventures to close down by January 2018, applying recently passed UN sanctions.

29 Sep 2017. Reports say that the Interpol General Assembly accepted the Palestinian Authority as a member.

30 Sep 2017. US Secretary of State Rex Tillerson met President Xi Jinping, and top Chinese diplomats in Beijing, on Saturday, 30 Sep, to discuss the North Korean nuclear crisis.

Researchers in Germany have demonstrated that hematopoietic stem cell (HSC) transplants can be improved by treatments that temporarily prevent the stem cells from dying. – The Rockefeller University Press

Doctors can now predict the severity of a disease by measuring molecules. The simple new technique could offer vastly superior predictions of disease severity in a huge range of conditions with a genetic component, including Alzheimer's, autism, cancer, cardiovascular disease, diabetes, obesity, schizophrenia and depression. – University of Virginia Health System.

Study of over 6000 people found that those between 45 and 84, whose arteries were free of calcium deposits, had a less than 3% chance of heart attack or stroke over the next decade--even if they had other risk factors, such as diabetes, high blood pressure, or high levels of bad cholesterol.

October 4th 2017 marks the 60th anniversary of the launch of Sputnik, the first manmade satellite, an event which marked the beginning of the Space Age.

Gallium is a metallic element that is used to make semiconductors, integrated circuits, transistors and solar cells.

Chicago 1837, in 2013: Chicago 'L' (elevated train 1892) on South Wabash Ave, with Trump Int. Tower (2009, 98 fl, 423 m, back).

Chapter 10. October 2017

1 Oct 2017. Vladimir Putin sent a message of congratulations to President of the People's Republic of China, Xi Jinping, on the 68th anniversary of the country's founding.
Note: Historians mention that after the end of World War II (September 1945), the U.S. continued their military assistance to Chiang Kai-shek (1887 – 1975, aged 87.4), and his KMT government forces, against the People's Liberation Army (PLA) led by Mao Zedong (26 Dec 1893 – 9 Sep 1976, aged 82.7), during the Chinese civil war. Likewise, Stalin (18 Dec 1878 – 5 March 1953, aged 74.2) gave quasi-covert support to Mao, by his occupation of north east China, which allowed the PLA to move in en masse, and take large supplies of arms left by the Japanese's Kwantung Army. Stalin annexed the Baltic states, and imposed the establishment of pro-Soviet Communist governments throughout Eastern Europe, as well as in China, North Korea and North Vietnam. With the approval and strong support of Stalin, Mao, 55, established the People's Republic of China on October 1, 1949. Then Mao (8 days before his 56th birthday) went to thank Joseph Stalin, and participated at Stalin's 71st birthday celebration in Moscow, on 18 December 1949.

2 Oct 2017. The White House. President Trump and Prime Minister Prayut Chan-o-Cha of Thailand had a bilateral meeting.

2 Oct 2017. The Russian President arrived in Turkmenistan at the invitation of President of Turkmenistan Gurbanguly Berdimuhamedov.
Vladimir Putin's official visit to Turkmenistan will include talks, which will focus on the key issues of developing bilateral cooperation in the political, trade, economic, scientific, education, culture and humanitarian fields, plus current regional issues.
Following the consultations, a package of Russian-Turkmenistani cooperation documents will be signed.

2 Oct 2017. Reports say that President Trump tweeted over the weekend "I told Rex Tillerson... that he is wasting his time trying to negotiate with Little Rocket Man," after the Secretary of State

acknowledged that the U.S. is in direct contact with North Korea. "Being nice to Rocket Man hasn't worked in 25 years, why would it work now? Clinton failed, Bush failed, and Obama failed. I won't fail." Many analysts say that this is not helpful for finding a peaceful solution.

Many analysts say that restrictions on good quality imports would hurt American consumers, because would create less innovation and higher prices.

2 Oct 2017. Vladimir Putin sent a message of condolences to President of the United States Donald Trump on the tragedy in Las Vegas. "The crime that took the lives of dozens of civilians is shocking in its cruelty," the Russian head of state wrote in the message. Vladimir Putin conveyed words of sympathy and support to the families and friends of the victims, and wished a speedy recovery to the injured.

5 Oct 2017. Vladimir Putin held talks with King Salman bin Abdulaziz Al Saud (81) of Saudi Arabia, who is in Russia on a state visit.
The two sides discussed a broad range of issues of Russian-Saudi cooperation, and prospects of enhancing bilateral cooperation in the trade, economic, investment, cultural and humanitarian areas. They also exchanged views on international issues.
A package of documents was signed following the talks.

5 Oct 2017. Vladimir Putin held talks with President of the Bolivarian Republic of Venezuela Nicolas Maduro in the Kremlin. Bilateral cooperation, as well as political, trade and economic issues, were discussed.

6 Oct 2017. The White House. President Donald J. Trump spoke today with President Emmanuel Macron of France. The two leaders discussed joint counterterrorism operations in the Sahel region of Africa, to defeat al-Qa'ida and other terrorist groups.

6 Oct 2017. The White House. President Donald J. Trump met with U.S. Ambassador to Russia Jon Huntsman Jr. (57), and his

wife, Mary Kaye Huntsman, to wish them well as they return to Moscow to represent the United States, and work toward improving our relationship with Russia.

6 Oct 2017. President Vladimir Putin (65 on 7 Oct) had a telephone conversation with President of Finland Sauli Niinisto, at the initiative of the Finnish side.
The discussion focused on topical matters of developing Russia–Finland relations, including cooperation in trade, the economy, as well as cultural and humanitarian projects.

10 Oct 2017. Reports say that Puerto Rico (population: 3.4 M U.S. citizens) is in a devastated state, with 80% of its agriculture destroyed, only 15% of the hospitals with electricity, and nearly half the population without potable water. While the federal government issued a 10-day waiver of the Jones Act to aid disaster relief efforts for the island, it expired on Sunday 8 Oct. The recent hurricane has highlighted why protectionist policies are costly in the best of times, and potentially devastating in the worst of times. Temporarily waiving such policies is not enough. Instead, it is time to end the Jones Act altogether.

10 Oct 2017. Vladimir Putin met with President of Tajikistan, Emomali Rahmon, in his Sochi residence, Bocharov Ruchei.

10 Oct 2017. Many experts and politicians say that high debt levels - attributable to the loose monetary policies (printing too much money) of central banks across the world, which were adopted in response to the global financial crisis in 2008 - present a threat to the global economy.

11 Oct 2017. The White House. President Donald J. Trump spoke today with Prime Minister Theresa May of the United Kingdom, to address ways to deny Iran all paths to a nuclear weapon.

11 Oct 2017. Vladimir Putin met with President of Uzbekistan, Shavkat Mirziyoyev (60). The meeting was held in Sochi ahead of the CIS summit.

11 Oct 2017. Ahead of the CIS summit that begins in Sochi today, Vladimir Putin met with President of Turkmenistan Gurbanguly Berdimuhamedov, to discuss bilateral relations.

11 Oct 2017. President of Russia chaired a meeting of the CIS Council of Heads of State in Sochi.
The summit was attended by President of Russia Vladimir Putin, President of Armenia Serzh Sargsyan, President of Azerbaijan Ilham Aliyev, President of Belarus Alexander Lukashenko, President of Kazakhstan Nazarbayev Nursultan, Prime Minister of Kyrgyzstan Sapar Isakov (40), President of Moldova Igor Dodon, President of Tajikistan Rahmon Emomali, President of Turkmenistan Gurbanguly Berdimuhamedov, President of Uzbekistan Shavkat Mirziyoyev, and Chairman of the CIS Executive Committee and CIS Executive Secretary Sergei Lebedev

11 Oct 2017. Vladimir Putin met with President of Moldova Igor Dodon in Sochi. The discussion focused, in particular, on topical issues of Russia-Moldova relations and possible ways of settling the Transnistria conflict.

11 Oct 2017. Vladimir Putin met in Sochi with President of Kazakhstan, Nursultan Nazarbayev. The Presidents discussed the status of bilateral relations, and topical international issues, particularly, the prospects of the Astana talks on conflict settlement in Syria.

Reports say that China this summer has made substantial progress in further establishing de facto control over most of the South China Sea.

11 Oct 2017. Xinhua China and Russia reaffirmed their positions on achieving denuclearization on the Korean Peninsula during a dialogue on Northeast Asian security, a Chinese Foreign Ministry spokesperson said Wednesday. Chinese Assistant Foreign

Minister Kong Xuanyou and Russian Deputy Foreign Minister Igor Morgulov Tuesday jointly chaired the eighth China-Russia consultation on the security situation in Northeast Asia, and discussed issues including the Korean Peninsula.

12 Oct 2017. The White House. President Trump (71) and First Lady Melania Trump (47, from Slovenia) greeted Prime Minister Justin Trudeau (45) of Canada and Mrs. Grégoire Trudeau (42) on the South Portico of the White House yesterday.

12 Oct 2017. Xinhua. The Chinese Defense Ministry on Wednesday, 11 Oct, voiced strong opposition to the unauthorized entry of a U.S. warship into China's waters off the Xisha Islands, in the South China Sea. The Chinese navy dispatched a missile frigate, two fighter jets, and a helicopter to warn the U.S. ship away, the ministry said in a statement. The U.S. navy missile destroyer Chafee entered China's territorial waters near the Xisha islands on Tuesday, 10 Oct, said the ministry, adding the provocation infringed upon China's sovereignty and security, harmed mutual trust between the two armies, as well as regional stability. The Chinese military will further strengthen its naval and air defense capability, to safeguard its sovereignty and security, according to the statement.
"It is a critical stage for the development of the relationship between Chinese and American armies, and we demand the U.S. side earnestly take steps to correct its mistakes, and inject positive energy into bilateral ties," the ministry said.

16 Oct 2017. Reports say that the latest election news coming out of Austria was: 31-year-old Sebastian Kurz has declared victory for his People's Party, setting him up to become Europe's youngest leader, and putting the country on course for a rightward turn. Austria's stock exchange ATX has so far returned 27% YTD, making it the continent's best-performing developed stock market this year.

16 Oct 2017. Vladimir Putin sent a message of greetings to Sooronbay Jeenbekov (58) on his election as President of the Kyrgyz Republic.

16 Oct 2017. Vladimir Putin has extended his condolences to President Mohamed Abdullahi Mohamed (55) of Somalia over the tragic consequences of the terrorist attack committed in the Somalian capital.

17 Oct 2017. White House. Today's dangerously flawed district court order undercuts the President's efforts to keep the American people safe, and enforce minimum security standards for entry into the United States. The Department of Justice will vigorously defend the President's lawful action. The proclamation restricting travel was issued after an extensive worldwide security review by the Secretary of Homeland Security, and following consultation by the President with members of the Cabinet, including the Secretaries of Homeland Security, State, and Defense and the Attorney General. The entry restrictions in the proclamation apply to countries based on their inability or unwillingness to share critical information necessary to safely vet applications, as well as a threat assessment related to terrorism, instability, and other grave national security concerns. These restrictions are vital to ensuring that foreign nations comply with the minimum security standards required for the integrity of our immigration system, and the security of our Nation. We are therefore confident that the Judiciary will ultimately uphold the President's lawful and necessary action, and swiftly restore its vital protections for the safety of the American people.

17 Oct 2017. The situation on the Korean Peninsula "has reached the touch-and-go point, and a nuclear war may break out any moment," according to North Korea's deputy U.N. ambassador. The warning from Kim In Ryong, which builds on previous escalating threats, comes as the U.S. and South Korea begin one of the largest joint naval drills in the region.

17 Oct 2017. Reports say that a new book about Gorbachev explains how a peasant boy turned into the Soviet system's gravedigger, why the Communist regime allowed him to destroy it, why Gorbachev's dream of democratizing the USSR did not work too well, how he and President Ronald Reagan turned out to be

almost perfect allies, and why Gorbachev permitted Eastern Europe to abandon Communism without firing a shot (except Romania).

18 Oct 2017. Reports say that President Trump has reiterated U.S. support for "responsible debt relief" for Greece after meeting with Prime Minister Alexis Tsipras (43) at the White House.

18 Oct 2017. White House. President Donald J. Trump spoke today with President Mauricio Macri of Argentina. The two leaders underscored their continued commitment to expanding trade and investment between the United States and Argentina.

18 Oct 2017. Vladimir Putin had a telephone conversation with Prime Minister of Israel, Benjamin Netanyahu, at the Israeli side's initiative.
The two leaders discussed Russian-Israeli cooperation in the context of the agreements they reached in Sochi on August 23.
They also spoke about the Syrian settlement, the Iranian nuclear programme, as well as the results of a recent referendum in the Kurdistan Region of Iraq.

18 Oct 2017. President Vladimir Putin held talks with President of the Republic of Croatia, Kolinda Grabar-Kitarovic, who is in Russia on an official visit at the invitation of the Russian leader.

18 Oct 2017. Reports say that Chinese President Xi Jinping opened a critical Communist Party Congress today, with a pledge to build a "modern socialist country" that will remain open to the world. The nation will also push ahead with market-oriented reforms of its foreign exchange rate, as well as its financial system, and let the market play a decisive role in the allocation of resources. The twice-a-decade meeting will run for a week until Oct. 24.

20 Oct 2017. North Korea is likely just "months away" from being capable of striking the U.S. with a nuclear missile, CIA Director Mike Pompeo (53) warned at a forum in Washington, stating that he's "deeply worried." "Accept and deter is unacceptable," National Security Adviser Gen. H.R. McMaster (55)

said at the same event. "We're not out of time but we're running out of time."

21 Oct 2017. Vladimir Putin had a telephone conversation with President of the Republic of Turkey, Recep Tayyip Erdogan.

24 Oct 2017. White House. President of the United States of America Donald J. Trump hosted Prime Minister of the Republic of Singapore, Lee Hsien Loong, at the White House on October 23, 2017.

24 Oct 2017. Vladimir Putin met at the Kremlin with President of the Republic of Cyprus, Nicos Anastasiades (71), who is in Russia on a working visit, at the invitation of the Russian President.

25 Oct 2017. Xinhua. Soon after being re-elected general secretary of the Central Committee of the Communist Party of China (CPC), Xi Jinping on Wednesday presented the new CPC central leadership to the press and laid down a roadmap for the next five years.
Reports say that as China's Communist Party Congress wraps up in Beijing, President Xi Jinping broke with tradition by unveiling a new leadership lineup that included no clear potential heirs, raising the chances that he might seek to stay in office beyond 2022. A stronger Xi will now be able to push through bold economic and financial reforms, as he also enshrined his name and doctrine into the party's constitution.
Xi Jinping Thought elevates Marxism to a new stage. With evolution of the Xi Jinping Thought, the CPC has declared that socialism with Chinese characteristics has entered a new era.

25 Oct 2017. White House. President Donald J. Trump spoke today with President Xi Jinping of China, on the occasion of the closing of China's Party Congress, to welcome continued cooperation of the two countries in the years ahead. President Trump told President Xi he looks forward to visiting China in early November, and to advancing joint efforts to denuclearize North Korea.

26 Oct 2017. Vladimir Putin had a telephone conversation with Chinese President Xi Jinping.

Vladimir Putin cordially congratulated Xi Jinping on his reelection to the post of General Secretary of the Communist Party of China, and on the successful 19th party congress.

It was affirmed that the President of Russia and the CPC leaders elected at the congress will continue to work together to further develop friendly Russian-Chinese relations. These relations, as was stressed, have reached an unprecedented level.

The leaders agreed to meet in person in the first half of November, at the APEC Summit in Vietnam.

27 Oct 2017. Xinhua. Xi calls for building a strong army.

China's military should take solid steps toward a strong army as socialism with Chinese characteristics has entered a new era, said Xi Jinping, general secretary of the Central Committee of the Communist Party of China (CPC). Xi made the remarks when meeting senior military officers in Beijing Thursday.

Xi, also Chinese president and chairman of the Central Military Commission (CMC), urged the army to remain true to its original aspiration and keep its mission firmly in mind.

He asked the army to learn and implement the spirit of the 19th CPC National Congress, following the road of building a strong army with Chinese characteristics and promoting the modernization of national defense and the army.

"We should strive to fully transform the people's armed forces into a world-class military by the mid-21st century," Xi said.

Xi said that during the past five years, the CMC has endeavored to build an army that follows the command of the CPC, is capable of winning battles and has a fine style of work.

Reports say that South Korea and China have agreed to normalize relations almost a year after Beijing launched a punitive economic war against Seoul, over its decision to host a U.S.-operated missile shield.

28 Oct 2017. The report delivered by Xi Jinping, general secretary of the Communist Party of China (CPC) Central

Committee, to the 19th CPC National Congress on Oct 18, has been published by People's Publishing House.

The report, "Secure a decisive victory in building a moderately prosperous society in all respects and strive for the great success of socialism with Chinese characteristics for a new era," was available at Xinhua Bookstores across the country from Friday.

General Secretary of the Communist Party of China (CPC) Central Committee, Xi Jinping, has said that the study and implementation of the "spirit of the 19th CPC National Congress" is the "primary political task" for the Party and country from now on.

Reports say that Japan had a $69 B surplus with the U.S. last year.

28 Oct 2017. Reports say that Sens. Cruz (46, R-Tx) and Patrick Leahy (77, D-Vt.) wrote a letter last week to Apple CEO regarding reports that Apple has removed Virtual Private Network (VPN) applications (apps) from the version of Apple's App Store available to users in the People's Republic of China, and urged him to stop enabling the Great Firewall, China's internet censorship system, which stifles free speech, and internet freedom.

31 Oct 2017. White House. President Donald J. Trump spoke yesterday (30 Oct) with Prime Minister Shinzo Abe of Japan, to discuss President Trump's upcoming travel to Japan.

Canada, Niagara Falls: the American Falls (21-30 m drop, 290 m wide, left), and the Horseshoe Falls (in Canada, 53 m drop, 790 m wide, right), with a boat with tourists (left) and a rainbow.

Chapter 11. November 2017

1 Nov 2017. White House. Today, President Donald J. Trump spoke with Prime Minister Narendra Modi of India.

1 Nov 2017. Vladimir Putin had a bilateral meeting with President of the Islamic Republic of Iran, Hassan Rouhani, in Tehran. During his working visit to Iran, Vladimir Putin met with Supreme Leader and spiritual leader of the Islamic Republic of Iran, Ayatollah Ali Khamenei (78).
The conversation took place after the meeting between the Russian leader and President of Iran Hassan Rouhani.
Vladimir Putin met with President of the Republic of Azerbaijan, Ilham Aliyev, in Tehran. Tehran hosted a trilateral meeting between Vladimir Putin, President of Iran, Hassan Rouhani, and President of Azerbaijan, Ilham Aliyev.

2 Nov 2017. Vladimir Putin had a telephone conversation with President of France, Emmanuel Macron, at the initiative of the French side.
Vladimir Putin briefed Mr. Macron on the results of his visit to Iran. In this context, the leaders spoke in favor of implementing in good faith the Joint Comprehensive Plan of Action to resolve the situation around Iran's nuclear programme. The unacceptability of unilaterally revising this major agreement was underscored.

2 Nov 2017. Vladimir Putin had a telephone conversation with President of Kazakhstan, Nursultan Nazarbayev.
The two presidents discussed the results of the Seventh International Meeting on Syria that was held in Astana on October 30–31.

3 Nov 2017. President Trump has nominated Jerome Powell (64) to run the Federal Reserve, after February 2018.

4 Nov 2017. Xinhua. Chinese President Xi Jinping on Friday, 3 Nov, instructed the armed forces to improve their combat capability and readiness for war.

6 Nov 2017. Vladimir Putin sent a message of condolences to President of the United States Donald Trump on the tragedy in Texas.

7 Nov 2017. The White House. Today, the National Day for the Victims of Communism, marks 100 years since the Bolshevik Revolution took place in Russia. The Bolshevik Revolution gave rise to the Soviet Union, and its dark decades of oppressive communism, a political philosophy incompatible with liberty, prosperity, and the dignity of human life.

Over the past century, communist totalitarian regimes around the world have killed more than 100 millions of people, and subjected countless more to exploitation, violence, and untold devastation. These movements, under the false pretense of liberation, systematically robbed innocent people of their God-given rights of free worship, freedom of association, and countless other rights we hold sacrosanct. Citizens yearning for freedom were subjugated by the state through the use of coercion, violence, and fear.

Today, we remember those who have died, and all who continue to suffer under communism. In their memory, and in honor of the indomitable spirit of those who have fought courageously to spread freedom and opportunity around the world, our Nation reaffirms its steadfast resolve to shine the light of liberty for all, who yearn for a brighter, freer future.

7 Nov 2017. Vladimir Putin instructed the Government to render humanitarian assistance to the Socialist Republic of Vietnam, and provide financial assistance in the amount of $5 M.

Vladimir Putin instructed the Government to carry out humanitarian operations. Vladimir Puchkov reported that an Il-76 aircraft is preparing to leave for Vietnam with humanitarian aid. The President also issued instructions to provide financial assistance to Vietnam in the amount of $5 M. The Russian leader expressed hope that other countries, planning to attend the APEC CEO Summit in Vietnam, would also show solidarity with the people of Vietnam.

A recent typhoon, which battered central Vietnam, was the most devastating natural disaster in two decades, leaving more than 60 dead, dozens missing, and damaging about 80,000 buildings. More than 40,000 people were evacuated.

8 Nov 2017: Reports say that China has a massive trade surplus with the U.S., which reached $26.62 B in October 2017.

8 Nov 2017. Reports say that Iranian President Hassan Rouhani has called the missile attacks on Riyadh (Saudi Arabia) by Yemen's Houthis a reaction to "Saudi aggression", and said the kingdom was making a "strategic mistake" by considering the U.S. a friend and Iran an enemy. The White House condemned the launch, saying Tehran "enabled" the attacks, which threatened regional security and "undermined" UN efforts to end the conflict.

9 Nov 2017. Reports: "Right now, unfortunately, the economic playing field is very unfair and one-sided. But, I don't blame China... I give China great credit," President Trump said in China, alongside President Xi Jinping. "In actuality, I blame past U.S. administrations to allow this out of control trade deficit to take place and to grow." He also discussed North Korea's nuclear and missile programs, stating, "China can fix this problem quickly and easily."

9 Nov 2017. The White House. President Trump (71) and President Xi (64) of China had a State Dinner in Beijing, China, Great Hall of the People. 6:36 P.M. CST (China Standard Time).

9 Nov 2017. The White House. President Trump and President Xi of China had a Joint Press Statement in Beijing, China, Great Hall of the People. 12:57 P.M. CST.

9 Nov 2017. Xinhua presentation of Trump visit. "China is willing to work together with the United States to respect each other, seek mutual benefit and reciprocity, focus on cooperation, and manage and control differences," Xi said during talks with visiting U.S. President Donald Trump. Since Wednesday (8 Nov) afternoon, the two presidents have had in-depth exchanges of views on bilateral ties and issues of common concern, and reached broad consensus, he said. "We believe Sino-U.S. relations concern not only the well-being of both peoples, but also world peace, prosperity and stability," Xi said. The presidents agreed that cooperation is the

"only correct choice" for China and the United States, and a better future would only be achieved through win-win cooperation, according to Xi. They agreed to maintain the leading role of head-of-state diplomacy in developing bilateral relations, Xi noted.

The two sides agreed to increase exchanges at various levels, give a full play to the four high-level dialogue mechanisms -- the diplomatic and security dialogue, the comprehensive economic dialogue, the law enforcement and cybersecurity dialogue, and the social and people-to-people dialogue, Xi said. They also agreed to expand cooperation in areas such as trade, the military, law enforcement and people-to-people exchanges, among others.

Both sides agreed to strengthen communication and coordination on issues involving the Korean Peninsula and Afghanistan. "There can be no more important subjects than China-U.S. relations," Trump said at the talks. "We have a capacity to solve world problems for many years to come."

9 Nov 2017. The White House. President Donald J. Trump Proclaims November 9, 2017, as World Freedom Day.

This World Freedom Day, 28 years after the fall of the Berlin Wall, we celebrate the day on November 9, 1989, when people of East and West Germany tore down the Berlin Wall and freedom triumphed over Communism.

On World Freedom Day, we recommit to the advancement of freedom over the forces of repression and radicalism. We continue to make clear that oppressive regimes should trust their people, and grant their citizens the liberty they deserve. The world will be better for it.

History: Straining through Soviet frequency jammers, Radio Free Europe (founded by the USA in 1949, and still functioning, now from Prague, Czech Republic) service broadcasters waged an ethereal Cold War battle from Munchen (West Germany), breaking through information barriers to connect with Eastern Europe dissidents, and feed popular independence revolutions across the Communist countries. In retrospect, these broadcasts would turn out to be some of the most impactful within the Soviet Block, though their existence was hard-fought, and far from guaranteed. Many people from Eastern Europe are very grateful for the very useful information received, during the Communist dictatorship, from Radio Free Europe.

9 Nov 2017. The White House. Today at the White House, Vice President Mike Pence met with Turkish Prime Minister Binali Yildirim (62) to reaffirm the enduring strategic partnership between the United States and Turkey. The Vice President expressed deep concern over the arrests of American citizens, Mission Turkey local staff, journalists, and members of civil society under the state of emergency, and urged transparency and due process in the resolution of their cases.

9 Nov 2017. Vladimir Putin met with President of the Republic of Kazakhstan, Nursultan Nazarbayev, in Chelyabinsk, Russia. The leaders of the two countries discussed urgent bilateral and international issues.

10 Nov 2017. White House. Presidential Proclamation Commemorating the 50th Anniversary of the Vietnam War.
We salute our brave Vietnam veterans who, in service to our Nation and in defense of liberty, fought gallantly against the spread of communism, and defended the freedom of the Vietnamese people

Report: Countries with the worst external debt: US ($18.6 T), UK ($7.8 T), France ($5.3 T), Germany ($5.1 T).

10 Nov 2017. Danang, Vietnam. Vladimir Putin met with President of the People's Republic of China, Xi Jinping, on the sidelines of the APEC Economic Leaders' Meeting in Danang.

10 Nov 2017. Danang, Vietnam. The President of Russia met with Prime Minister of Japan, Shinzo Abe, on the sidelines of the APEC Economic Leaders' Meeting in Danang. Abe noted: It is nice to know that we are meeting for the 20th time today.

10 Nov 2017. Vladimir Putin met with President of the Socialist Republic of Vietnam, Tran Dai Quang, on the sidelines of the APEC Economic Leaders' Meeting in Danang. The two leaders discussed issues of bilateral cooperation.

10 Nov 2017. Danang, Vietnam. Vladimir Putin and President of the Philippines Rodrigo Duterte met on the sidelines of the two-day APEC Economic Leaders' Meeting, which opened today in Danang, Vietnam.

10 Nov 2017. Xinhua. Journalists from across China have said they were inspired by Chinese President Xi Jinping's remarks on journalism, and would endeavor to spread China's voice.
Xi, also general secretary of the Communist Party of China (CPC) Central Committee, called on journalists to "strengthen their confidence in the path, theory, system, and culture of socialism with Chinese characteristics."

11 Nov 2017. Danang, Vietnam. President of Russia Vladimir Putin (65) and President of the United States Donald Trump (71) approved a joint statement on Syria, following a conversation on the sidelines of the APEC Economic Leaders' Meeting. The document had been drafted by the two countries' experts, and coordinated by the Russian Foreign Minister Sergei Lavrov and US Secretary of State Rex Tillerson. The statement has been specially prepared for the Danang meeting.
Vladimir Putin and Donald Trump had a conversation before the group photo ceremony for the APEC Economic Leaders.

11 Nov 2017. Xinhua. Chinese President Xi Jinping and his Chilean counterpart Michelle Bachelet (66) witness the signing of a bilateral deal on upgrading the Free Trade Agreement (FTA) between the two countries in Da Nang, Vietnam, Nov. 11, 2017.
Xi underlined that this is China's first FTA upgrade completed with a Latin American country.

11 Nov 2017. Danang, Vietnam. The 25th APEC Economic Leaders' Meeting ended in Danang.

12 Nov 2017. Xinhua. Chinese President Xi Jinping, who is also general secretary of the Communist Party of China (CPC) Central Committee, arrived in the Vietnamese capital of Hanoi on Sunday, 12 Nov, for a state visit to the Southeast Asian country

(after President Trump). It is Xi's second visit to Vietnam as China's head of state and top CPC leader. His previous state visit was in 2015. Before flying to Hanoi, Xi concluded a busy two-day stay in Vietnam's central city of Da Nang, where he attended the 25th Asia-Pacific Economic Cooperation (APEC) Economic Leaders' Meeting. The fact that China and Vietnam both follow the leadership of Communist parties and socialist road, jointly strengthen solidarity and cooperation, as well as seek prosperity, is in line with the fundamental interests of both peoples and conducive to the peace, stability and development of the region and the world, said Xi. Xi urged the two countries continue to be good neighbors, good friends, good comrades and good partners.

Trong, on behalf of the Vietnamese party, government and people, extended warm welcome to Xi, saying that Vietnam and China are neighbors with traditional friendship. Xi said that the two countries should properly manage differences, protect maritime peace and stability, and promote joint exploitation.

China and Vietnam are socialist neighboring countries and important cooperative partners, and the fate of the two parties, two countries and two peoples are closely bound up together with the same political systems and development goals, Xi said.

13 Nov 2017. White House. At the invitation of the President of the Socialist Republic of Vietnam, Tran Dai Quang, President Donald J. Trump paid a state visit to Hanoi, Vietnam, this weekend, from November 11 to12, 2017 (before President Xi).

Both leaders pledged to deepen and expand the bilateral trade and investment relationship between the United States and Vietnam, and reaffirmed their commitment to promote peace, cooperation, prosperity, and security in the Indo-Pacific region. Reports say that President Trump has offered to help resolve territorial disputes in the South China Sea, telling Vietnam's President Tran Dai Quang over the weekend, "if I can help mediate or arbitrate, please let me know." Affirming their commitment to deepened defense cooperation and shared resolve to address regional security challenges, President Quang thanked the United States Government for the transfer of a Hamilton-class Coast Guard cutter to help improve Vietnam's maritime security and law enforcement capabilities. Both leaders welcomed the plan for the first ever visit, in 2018, by a United States aircraft carrier to a Vietnamese port.

13 Nov 2017. Manila. Trump extended his Asian tour by one day to attend the start of the 12th East Asia Summit Head of State and Government (19 countries: Australia, Brunei, Cambodia, Canada, China, India, Indonesia, Japan, Laos, Malaysia, Myanmar, New Zealand, Philippines, Russia, Singapore, South Korea, Thailand, United States, Vietnam; 4 guest invitees: East Timor, European Union, Chile, United Nations) Luncheon at the Philippine International Convention Center in Manila, Philippines.

13 Nov 2017. The White House. President Donald J. Trump met today with Prime Minister Narendra Modi of India in Manila, Philippines.

13 Nov 2017. The White House. President Donald J. Trump met with Prime Minister Malcolm Turnbull of Australia, and Prime Minister Shinzo Abe of Japan today in Manila, Philippines.

13 Nov 2017. The White House. U.S. President Donald J. Trump and Philippine President Rodrigo Duterte met in Manila, Philippines on November 13, 2017, to discuss a broad range of shared interests and priorities.

13 Nov 2017. The White House. Today, Vice President Mike Pence welcomed to the White House Secretary of State Cardinal Pietro Parolin, to reaffirm the strong and enduring cooperation between the United States and the Holy See.

13 Nov 2017. Xinhua. Chinese President Xi Jinping, also general secretary of the Communist Party of China (CPC) Central Committee, arrived in Laos Monday, 13 Nov, for a state visit as the two socialist countries are seeking to consolidate their traditional friendship.

13 Nov 2017. Vladimir Putin received President of Turkey Recep Tayyip Erdogan at the Bocharov Ruchei residence in Sochi.

The President of Turkey arrived in Sochi for a working visit at the invitation of the President of Russia.
Mr. Putin and Mr. Erdogan exchanged opinions on regional and international issues, including the joint fight against terrorism and the situation with the Syrian peace settlement.

13 Nov 2013. Vladimir Putin has expressed his condolences to President of Iraq, Fuad Masum (79), on the tragic consequences of the earthquake in Sulaymaniyah Province. This disastrous earthquake occurred on November 12 on the border between Iran and Iraq.

13 Nov 2017. 23 EU governments (Austria, Belgium, Bulgaria, Croatia, Republic of Cyprus, Czech Republic, Estonia, Finland, France, Germany, Greece, Hungary, Italy, Latvia, Lithuania, Luxembourg, Netherlands, Poland, Romania, Slovakia, Slovenia, Spain, Sweden) signed a defense pact today, marking a new era of European military integration. The effort was long blocked by Britain, which feared the creation of an EU army, but it took off after Brexit, the election of pro-European Emmanuel Macron, and warnings from President Trump that European allies must pay more towards their security. The pact includes all EU governments except Britain, which is leaving the bloc, Denmark, which has opted out of defense matters, Ireland, Portugal and Malta. Traditionally neutral Austria was a late addition to the pact.

History report: The collapse of the European communism in 1989, due to Gorbachev (86), shocked the international system. In that perilous moment, Germany reunified, Saddam Hussein of Iraq chose to invade Kuwait, China cracked down on pro-democracy protesters, under Gorbachev the Soviet Union ceased to exist, and regimes throughout Eastern Europe teetered between democratic change, and new authoritarians. Facing more international crises in his single White House term, than any Oval Office occupant since Franklin Roosevelt at the height of World War II, George H.W. Bush (93) faced a world in turmoil that might easily have tipped into an epic crisis. It did not, in large measure because of his quiet collaboration with Gorbachev, and because of his recognition that tense moments required calm words, and that international crises are best handled behind closed doors. Bush did not end the Cold War. Gorbachev did. And they did everything to keep its end surprisingly peaceful.

Reports: Norway's $1 T sovereign wealth fund is the world's largest.

15 Nov 2017. Xinhua. California Governor Jerry Brown (79), speaking in Bonn, Germany, on Nov. 14, said his state is counting on China to drive down the price of zero emission vehicles.

16 Nov 2017. Vladimir Putin met with President of Armenia, Serzh Sargsyan, at the Kremlin.

16 Nov 2017. Vladimir Putin had a telephone conversation with Head of the Donetsk People's Republic, Alexander Zakharchenko (41), and Head of the Lugansk People's Republic, Igor Plotnitsky (53). The discussion focused on the initiative put forward by Viktor Medvedchuk (63), the leader of the Ukrainian Choice – People's Right movement, on a prisoner exchange between Ukraine, and the Donetsk and Lugansk People's republics. The leaders of the Donetsk and Lugansk People's republics supported the initiative, and noted that the issue had to be discussed, and the details finalized, with representatives from the Ukrainian side.

17 Nov 2017. The White House. The United States expresses grave concern about the Cambodian government's dissolution of the country's main opposition party, the Cambodia National Rescue Party (CNRP), based on meritless and politicized allegations that it participated in a conspiracy to overthrow the government. It is becoming increasingly evident to the world that the Cambodian government's restrictions on civil society, suppression of the press, and banning of more than 100 opposition leaders from political activities have significantly set back Cambodia's democratic development, and placed its economic growth and international standing at risk. The United States will take concrete steps to respond to the Cambodian government's deeply regrettable actions. As a first step, we will terminate support for the Cambodian National Election Committee, and its administration of the

upcoming 2018 national election. On current course next year's election will not be legitimate, free, or fair. The Cambodian government still has time to reverse course. We call on the Royal Government of Cambodia to undo its recent actions against the CNRP, release imprisoned CNRP leader Kem Sokha, and allow opposition parties, civil society, and the media to maintain their legitimate activities.

17 Nov 2017. Xinhua. Chinese President Xi Jinping held talks with Panamanian President, Juan Carlos Varela, on Friday, 17 Nov, saying bilateral relations "turned over a new leaf" with the establishment of diplomatic relations. Varela is making his first state visit to China, after the Central American nation established diplomatic relations with China in June 2017.

17 Nov 2017. Xinhua. China's determination to deepen strategic cooperation with Saudi Arabia will not waver, no matter how the international and regional situation alters, Chinese President Xi Jinping told Saudi King Salman bin Abdulaziz Al Saud in his phone conversation with the ruler Thursday, 16 Nov.

17 Nov 2017. Vladimir Putin met with President of the Kyrgyz Republic, Almazbek Atambayev, who has arrived in Russia to take part in events of the St Petersburg International Cultural Forum.

20 Nov 2017. The White House. President Donald J. Trump spoke today with President Emmanuel Macron of France about the situation in Lebanon and Syria

20 Nov 2017. Reports from UN: The mandate of the joint Organization for the Prohibition of Chemical Weapons (OPCW)-UN panel, the Joint Investigative Mechanism (JIM) expires today. It was a draft resolution to maintain the JIM, but, in addition to the permanent member Russia, Bolivia voted against the draft. Another permanent member China abstained.

20 Nov 2017. Vladimir Putin had a telephone conversation with Emir of the State of Qatar, Tamim bin Hamad Al Thani.

20 Nov 2017. Reports: President Robert Mugabe (93) has been dismissed as leader of Zimbabwe's ruling ZANU-PF party, following a de facto military coup. He'll be replaced by the vice president he previously sacked, Emmerson Mnangagwa (75), who will focus on rebuilding ties with the outside world, and stabilizing an economy in free fall. Mugabe's removal is also likely to send similar political shockwaves across Africa.

21 Nov 2017. On November 20, President Vladimir Putin (65) had talks with President of the Syrian Arab Republic, Bashar al-Assad (52), who was in Russia on a working visit.

21 Nov 2017. The White House. President Donald J. Trump today spoke with President Vladimir V. Putin of Russia for more than one hour. The presidents affirmed their support for the Joint Statement of the United States and the Russian Federation, issued at the Asia-Pacific Economic Cooperation Summit on November 11. Both presidents also stressed the importance of implementing U.N. Security Council Resolution 2254, and supporting the U.N.-led Geneva Process to peacefully resolve the Syrian civil war, end the humanitarian crisis, allow displaced Syrians to return home, and ensure the stability of a unified Syria, free of malign intervention and terrorist safe havens.
The two presidents affirmed the importance of fighting terrorism together throughout the Middle East and Central Asia and agreed to explore ways to further cooperate in the fight against ISIS, al-Qaeda, the Taliban, and other terrorist organizations.
President Trump and President Putin also discussed how to implement a lasting peace in Ukraine, and the need to continue international pressure on North Korea to halt its nuclear weapon and missile programs.

21 Nov 2017. The Kremlin. As agreed in advance, Vladimir Putin had a telephone conversation with President of the United States of America, Donald Trump.
Current Syrian issues, in view of the military operation to destroy terrorists in Syria which is winding down, were thoroughly discussed. Vladimir Putin stressed Russia's willingness to actively

facilitate a durable political settlement in that country on the basis of UN Security Council Resolution 2254 and in keeping with the agreements reached as part of the Astana meetings and the provisions of the Joint Statement approved by the presidents of Russia and the United States on November 11 at the APEC Economic Leaders' Meeting in Vietnam. It was noted, in particular, that this statement met with a positive reaction in the Middle East.

There was discussion of the need to preserve the sovereignty, independence and territorial integrity of Syria, and to achieve a political settlement on the basis of principles that must be worked out as a result of the broadest possible intra-Syrian negotiation process. This is precisely the aim of Russia's initiative to hold the National Dialogue Conference in Sochi soon.

Vladimir Putin informed Donald Trump about the main outcomes of the November 20 meeting with Bashar al-Assad, where the Syrian leader reaffirmed his commitment to the political process, constitutional reform, and presidential and parliamentary elections. In addition, emphasis was placed on the upcoming trilateral talks in Sochi on November 22 with the participation of the presidents of Russia, Iran and Turkey, during which steps to further normalize the situation in Syria and various aspects of the political settlement process are to be coordinated.

More broadly, the President of Russia once again spoke in favor of joint antiterrorist efforts with the United States, noting the practical importance of coordinating efforts between the special services of both countries. The US President was supportive of this idea.

Vladimir Putin and Donald Trump also exchanged views on the current state of affairs on the Korean Peninsula, emphasizing that it would be advisable to find a negotiated solution to the problem by diplomatic means.

Regarding the crisis in southeast Ukraine, the President of Russia pointed to the lack of a real alternative to unconditional compliance with the Minsk agreements of February 12, 2015.

The two leaders touched on the situation in Afghanistan, which is of concern due to the growing terrorist and drug trafficking threats.

The situation surrounding the Iranian nuclear programme was also discussed. Russia's commitment to full implementation of the Joint Comprehensive Plan of Action was noted, as it is an essential factor

in ensuring regional stability and overcoming the challenge of non-proliferation of weapons of mass destruction.
Both sides expressed satisfaction with the businesslike and substantive conversation.

21 Nov 2017. Vladimir Putin held talks in Sochi with President of the Czech Republic, Milos Zeman (73), who is in Russia on an official visit.

21 Nov 2017. Vladimir Putin's telephone conversation with King of Saudi Arabia, Salman bin Abdulaziz Al Saud, focused on the progress toward implementing the agreements reached during the King's recent visit to Russia.

21 Nov 2017. Vladimir Putin had a telephone conversation with Prime Minister of Israel Benjamin Netanyahu, at the initiative of the Israeli side. The conversation included a substantive exchange on the prospects of developments in the Middle East, primarily in the context of the concluding stage of the fight against international terrorism in Syria.

21 Nov 2017. Vladimir Putin had a telephone conversation with President of the Arab Republic of Egypt Abdel Fattah el-Sisi.
Vladimir Putin gave the Egyptian leader a detailed account of Russian assessments of the latest developments in Syria in the context of the military operation to destroy terrorists in that country, which is nearing completion.

21 Nov 2017. Xinhua. President Xi Jinping called for nongovernmental organizations along the Silk Road to contribute to enhancing mutual understanding and friendship between people of different countries, promoting common development and building a community of shared future for mankind. He made the remark in a congratulatory message to the First Silk Road NGO Cooperation Network Forum, which started on Tuesday in Beijing and has drawn nearly 200 representatives from more than 50 countries.

22 Nov 2017.   Vladimir Putin held a meeting in Sochi (Russia) with President of Iran Hassan Rouhani, and President of Turkey Recep Tayyip Erdogan.

Following the meeting with the presidents of Iran and Turkey, Vladimir Putin held a separate bilateral meeting with President of Iran Hassan Rouhani.

23 Nov 2017. In the course of a telephone conversation with President of Argentina, Mauricio Macri, Vladimir Putin expressed his condolences over the situation with the San Juan submarine missing in the Atlantic Ocean. The President of Russia offered search and rescue assistance. The two leaders have agreed that their defense departments will maintain contact in this context.

They also discussed current aspects of the further development of Russian-Argentinean relations.

23 Nov 2017. In Sochi, Vladimir Putin held talks with President of the Republic of the Sudan, Omar Al-Bashir (73), who is currently in Russia on a working visit. During the consultations, the sides exchanged opinions on the development of Russian-Sudanese relations and topical international issues, including the situation in the Middle East and North Africa.

23 Nov 2017. At the Bocharov Ruchei residence in Sochi, Vladimir Putin received former Prime Minister of Italy, Romano Prodi (78), who is in Russia on a private visit.

23 Nov 2017. Reports: In 2017, Russian arms have been delivered to 59 countries. Stable military contracts have been concluded with 80 countries.

Reports: Egypt was hit by its deadliest ever terrorist attack this past weekend, after gunmen - linked to Islamic State - opened fire and set off explosives at a mosque in the Sinai Peninsula, killing more than 300 people.

24 Nov 2017. The White House. President Donald J. Trump spoke today with President Abdel Fattah Al Sisi of Egypt to offer

condolences to the people of Egypt, after the heinous attack on worshippers in Egypt's North Sinai province.

24 Nov 2017. China Daily. Premier Li Keqiang met with Djiboutian President Ismail Omar Guelleh (71) in Beijing.

25 Nov 2017. China Daily. The People Liberation Army (PLA) established its Djibouti Logistics Support Base, the first of its kind for the Chinese military, on July 11, and put it into formal operation on Aug 1. Located in Djibouti City, the African nation's capital, the base will support the Chinese military's naval escort, peacekeeping and humanitarian missions in Africa and western Asia, the Navy said. It will also help China improve its capabilities in international military cooperation, joint exercises, emergency evacuations and overseas rescue.
It will enable the nation to better guard the safety of international strategic maritime passages with other countries, it said.
President Xi Jinping, also chairman of the Central Military Commission (CMC), had a teleconference with troops at the Djibouti base this month, during an inspection of the CMC Joint Command Headquarters in Beijing. Xi told them to gain a good reputation for Chinese soldiers, and to contribute to regional peace and stability.

25 Nov 2017. Xinhua. China launched remote sensing satellites at 2:10 am, Beijing Time, Saturday 25 Nov, on a Long March-2C rocket, from Xichang Satellite Launch Center in southwest China's Sichuan Province.
The satellites have entered the preset orbit, and Saturday's launching mission was proclaimed a success. The satellites will conduct electromagnetic probes and other experiments.
The launch is the 256th mission of the Long March rocket family.

27 Nov 2017. The White House. President Donald J. Trump spoke today with President Emmanuel Macron of France. The presidents agreed on the importance of the United Nations-based Geneva Process as the only legitimate forum for achieving a political solution in Syria.

27 Nov. 2017. The White House. The United States strongly condemns the release of Lashkar-e-Tayyiba (LeT) leader Hafiz Saeed from house arrest in Pakistan, and calls for his immediate re-arrest and prosecution.

LeT is a designated Foreign Terrorist Organization responsible for the death of hundreds of innocent civilians in terrorist attacks, including a number of American citizens. Saeed himself is a notorious terrorist, who stands accused of having masterminded the November 2008 Mumbai attacks that killed 166 people, including six American citizens. A clear international consensus exists regarding Saeed's culpability—he was designated by the United Nations under U.N. Security Council Resolution 1267 in December 2008. The Department of the Treasury has designated Saeed as a Specially Designated Global Terrorist, and the United States, since 2012, has offered a $10 million reward for information that brings Saeed to justice. Saeed's release, after Pakistan's failure to prosecute or charge him, sends a deeply troubling message about Pakistan's commitment to combatting international terrorism, and belies Pakistani claims that it will not provide sanctuary for terrorists on its soil. If Pakistan does not take action to lawfully detain Saeed, and charge him for his crimes, its inaction will have repercussions for bilateral relations, and for Pakistan's global reputation.

28 Nov 2017, 3:41 PM. The White House. SECRETARY OF DEFENSE MATTIS: Mr. President, Senator, Speaker, a little over two and a half hours ago (12:48 PM, which in North Korea is 2:48 AM Thursday 29 Nov), North Korea launched an intercontinental ballistic missile. It went higher, frankly, than any previous shot they've taken. It's a research and development effort on their part, to continue building ballistic missiles that could threaten everywhere in the world, basically.

28 Nov 2017. The White House. President Donald J. Trump spoke today with President Moon Jae-in of the Republic of Korea, to discuss the alliance's response to North Korea's test of an intercontinental ballistic missile.

29 Nov 2017. Vladimir Putin met with Premier of the State Council of China, Li Keqiang (62), in the Kremlin.

29 Nov 2017. The White House. President Donald J. Trump spoke today with President Xi Jinping of the People's Republic of China, to discuss North Korea's latest missile launch. President Trump underscored the determination of the United States to defend ourselves, and our allies from the growing threat posed by the North Korean regime. President Trump emphasized the need for China to use all available levers to convince North Korea to end its provocations and return to the path of denuclearization.

29 Nov 2017. Vladimir Putin held talks in the Kremlin with President of the Kyrgyz Republic, Sooronbay Jeenbekov, who has arrived in Russia on a working visit.

29 Nov 2017. Vladimir Putin congratulated President of the State of Palestine, Mahmoud Abbas, on the International Day of Solidarity with the Palestinian People.

30 Nov 2017. Xinhua. Chinese President Xi Jinping told his U.S. counterpart, Donald Trump, in a telephone conversation late Wednesday, 29 Nov, that denuclearizing the Korean Peninsula, maintaining international nuclear-nonproliferation regime, and preserving peace and stability in Northeast Asia are China's unswerving goal. He said China would like to keep up communications with the United States and all other related parties, and jointly push the nuclear issue towards the direction of peaceful settlement via dialogues and negotiations. In response, Trump said the United States has serious concerns over the launch of a ballistic missile by the Democratic People's Republic of Korea (DPRK).
The DPRK's Korean Central Television reported that the country successfully test-fired a newly developed Intercontinental Ballistic Missile early Wednesday, 29 Nov, morning, a move that has drawn condemnation from the international community.

30 Nov 2017. The White House. President Donald J. Trump spoke today with President Moon Jae-in of the Republic of Korea for the second time since North Korea launched an intercontinental ballistic missile on November 28.

30 Nov 2017. The White House. President Trump had a meeting with Crown Prince Salman of Bahrain, in the Oval Office.

30 Nov 2017. Reports: The Trump administration has condemned China's bid for recognition as a market economy in the WTO, citing decades of legal precedent, and signs the country is moving in the opposite direction under Xi Jinping. The step by the U.S. came in a legal submission filed last week, and is due to be released publicly today, in a case brought by Beijing against the EU.

30 Nov 2017. Vladimir Putin arrived in Minsk, Belarus, on a working visit, which includes a meeting of the Collective Security Council of the Collective Security Treaty Organization.

30 Nov 2017. Xinhua. Chinese President Xi Jinping met with former U.S. President Barack Obama (56) in Beijing on Wednesday, 29 Nov, calling for enhanced communication, exchanges and cooperation between China and the United States.
Xi made a positive appraisal of Obama's efforts in promoting China-U.S. relations during his presidency.

30 Nov 2017. Xinhua. Russian military confirmed Tuesday, 28 Nov, that its warplane drove away a U.S. Navy aircraft last week over the Black Sea.
Russian air control detected a target rapidly approaching the Russian border over international waters of the Black Sea, on Nov. 25, said the press-service of Russia's Southern Military District.
A Su-30 fighter took off, approached the air target and identified it as a U.S. aircraft P-8A Poseidon, it said.
After spotting the Russian jet, the P-8A changed its route and flew away from the Russian border.
CNN reported Monday, 27 Nov, that a Russian Su-30 fighter made an "unsafe" intercept of a U.S. P-8A Poseidon aircraft Saturday, 25 Nov, while it was flying over the Black Sea.
The U.S. plane "was operating in international airspace, and did nothing to provoke this Russian behavior," a Pentagon representative was quoted by CNN as saying.

30 Nov 2017. Reports: The US Ambassador said at a 13th U.N. Security Council meeting on North Korea issue in 2017: "If war comes, the North Korean regime will be utterly destroyed." China's representative urged Pyongyang to stop all actions to escalate tensions on the Korean Peninsula. He recalled that his country and the Russian Federation had issued a joint statement offering a roadmap to resumed negotiations. They proposed suspending Korean nuclear activity, as well as large-scale joint military exercises involving the United States, in order to establish a political mechanism. Bolivia's delegate, alongside the representatives of Sweden and other countries, cautioned against any use of force, or threat to use force, in settling disputes, urging all to refrain from provocations. The Council's imposition of draconian sanctions on Pyongyang could not be an end in itself, but only a means to convince the concerned parties to sit down in dialogue, he said.

Paris in 2013: Place de la Concorde (1772): The Egyptian obelisk (Ramses the Great, 1250 BC, 23 m), Marine Nationale (1758, left).

Chapter 12. December 2017

1 Dec 2017. The White House. President Trump met with Libyan Prime Minister, Fayez al-Sarraj (57), at the White House today. He and the Libyan Prime Minister discussed ways to cooperate on counterterrorism, and expand bilateral engagement between the two countries.

1 Dec 2017. Xinhua. China will stick to its basic national policy of opening-up, and participate in global governance, with a more positive gesture, President Xi Jinping said on Thursday, 30 Nov. Xi made the remarks while meeting with representatives of the Imperial Springs International Forum at the Great Hall of the People in Beijing. The representatives (over 100) are mainly incumbent and former top leaders of foreign countries (including Mexico, Colombia, Bolivia, South Korea, Indonesia, Greece, Latvia, New Zealand, Australia, Finland, Romania, Italy, Sweden), and international organizations (Club de Madrid).
In 2016, the overall investment in renewable energy in China was $103 billions, which is more than the $49 billions of the European Union, and the $43 billions of the United States, he said, adding that the number of industrial robots made in China and working in China last year was 87,000 units, compared with Number 2 South Korea's 47,000 units, and Number 3 US' 40,000 units.

1 Dec 2017. Xinhua. Chinese President Xi Jinping, also general secretary of the Communist Party of China (CPC) Central Committee, said the CPC is willing to work with other political parties around the world, to promote the building of a community with a shared future for mankind, and create a better world.
Xi made the remarks while delivering a keynote speech on Friday, 1 Dec, at the opening ceremony of CPC in Dialogue with World Political Parties High-Level Meeting in Beijing. The meeting was attended by leaders from nearly 300 parties and political organizations from more than 120 countries and regions.

1 Dec 2017. Reports: The Hwasong-15 missile that North Korea launched on Wednesday, 29 Dec, which reached an altitude

of 4,474 km, is a new type of ICBM that can fly over 13,000 km, a South Korean defense ministry spokesman told Reuters. The missile traveled 950 km in 53 minutes before splashing down into the Sea of Japan.

3 Dec 2017. Xinhua Chinese President Xi Jinping sent a congratulatory letter to the Fourth World Internet Conference, which opened Sunday, 3 Dec, in east China's watertown of Wuzhen. The conference from Sunday to Tuesday is themed on "Developing digital economy for openness and shared benefits -- building a community of common future in cyberspace."

Reports: at the International Robot Exhibition in Tokyo. Toyota has showcased a humanoid robot that can mirror its user's movements, a product it says has uses as varied as elderly care and disaster response. The T-HR3 can be controlled by a wearable system that allows users to operate the entire robot in real time by simply moving their own limbs.

4 Dec 2017. The White House. President Donald J. Trump spoke today with President Emmanuel Macron of France. The Presidents agreed on the need for the Iraqi government and the Kurdistan Regional Government to resolve their differences through dialogue.

4 Dec 2017. Xinhua. Chinese President Xi Jinping said China hopes to encourage countries around the world to take a ride on the express train of internet and digital economic development.
Xi, also general secretary of the Communist Party of China (CPC) Central Committee, made the remarks in a congratulatory letter to the Fourth World Internet Conference, which opened Sunday, 3 Dec, in the east China town of Wuzhen.
Over 1,500 guests from more than 80 countries and regions, including government representatives, heads of international organizations, leading figures of internet companies, online celebrities, experts and scholars, attended the conference.
Reports: Press freedom, human rights, and people's liberty groups expressed concerns about all these conferences, which only

aim to promote China's policies, and some Chinese, persecuted for their insistence to have some political freedom, peacefully protested.

4 Dec 2017. Vladimir Putin had a telephone conversation with President of Kazakhstan Nursultan Nazarbayev.
The two leaders discussed a number of current matters taking into account the results of the Collective Security Treaty Organization Collective Security Council meeting, which was held on November 30 in Minsk.

4 Dec 2017. Vladimir Putin had a telephone conversation with President of the Arab Republic of Egypt Abdel Fattah el-Sisi.

4 Dec 2017. The Kremlin. After the meeting with the heads of delegations of the local Orthodox churches, Vladimir Putin met with Patriarch John of Antioch and All the East (62), from Syria.

4 Dec 2017. Reports: Trade will be high on the agenda this week as Canadian Prime Minister Justin Trudeau visits China in a bid to boost business ties with the world's second-largest economy. Canada has previously explored opening full-blown free trade talks with China, and Trudeau's Dec. 3-7 trip comes as he struggles with trade pacts in North America, and with other partners in Asia.

4 Dec 2017. Reports: Just a week after North Korea test-fired its most advanced ICBM, South Korea and the U.S. have launched their annual aerial drills, which Pyongyang said would push the "peninsula to the brink of nuclear war." Called Vigilant Ace, the program will run until Friday, 8 Dec, with six F-22 Raptor stealth fighters to be deployed among more than 230 aircraft.

4 Dec 2017. Reports: Saudi Arabia's sentiment was helped by hopes for an end to the conflict in Yemen. Former Yemeni President Ali Abdullah Saleh (70.7), previously allied with Houthi forces, said he was ready for a "new page" in ties with the Saudi-led coalition fighting in Yemen, if the kingdom stopped attacks on his country.

5 Dec 2017. Reports: Saudi Arabian warplanes have bombed the presidential palace in Yemen's capital, stepping up attacks on Houthi rebels, after they killed ex-President Ali Abdullah Saleh (70.7), just as he appeared set to switch sides in the conflict. His death may alter the course of the war in the country, and comes as the U.S. Supreme Court upheld President Trump's travel ban on six Muslim-majority nations, including Yemen.

5 Dec 2017. The White House. President Donald J. Trump spoke separately today with Prime Minister Benjamin Netanyahu of Israel, President Mahmoud Abbas of the Palestinian Authority, His Majesty King Abdullah II of Jordan, President Abdel Fattah Al Sisi of Egypt, and His Majesty King Salman Bin Abdulaziz Al Saud of Saudi Arabia.

5 Dec 2017. The Kremlin. Vladimir Putin had a telephone conversation with President of the State of Palestine, Mahmoud Abbas, at the latter's initiative.
During the discussion of the Middle East settlement process, Vladimir Putin stated Russia's principled stand in support of the immediate resumption of direct Palestinian-Israeli talks on all disputed issues, including the status of Jerusalem, with a view to making long-term and fair decisions in the interests of both countries. The importance of the agreement between Fatah and Hamas to bolster Palestinian unity, signed in Cairo in October 2017, was noted. Current issues of bilateral cooperation were discussed in the context of the agreements reached during the Russian-Palestinian summit in Moscow, in May 2017.
The two presidents agreed to maintain personal contact.

5 Dec 2017. Reports. UN chief diplomat Jeffrey Feltman (58) travels to North Korea today for rare, high-level, political talks.

5 Dec 2017. King Mihai I passed away on 5 Dec 2017, at 96 years 1 month and 10 days. He reigned as King of Romania from 20 July 1927 to 8 June 1930, and again from 6 September 1940 until his forced abdication on 30 December 1947.

6 Dec 2017. The White House. President Donald J. Trump is following through on his promise to recognize Jerusalem as the capital of the State of Israel, and has instructed the State Department to begin to relocate the U.S. Embassy to Israel from Tel Aviv to Jerusalem.

6 Dec 2017. Vladimir Putin sent a message of greetings to the President of the Republic of Finland on Independence Day, the country's national holiday.

6 Dec 2017. Vladimir Putin: I will be a candidate for the office of President of the Russian Federation.

7 Dec 2017. Xinhua. Chinese President Xi Jinping Wednesday, 6 Dec, told world business leaders gathering in China that the country would continue to open up and improve its business climate, to create more opportunities and make a greater contribution to the world. Xi made the remarks in a congratulatory letter to the 2017 Fortune Global Forum, which opened in the southern China city of Guangzhou Wednesday.
The three-day 2017 Fortune Global Forum has chosen "Openness and Innovation: Shaping the Global Economy" as its theme, drawing 1,100 participants, mostly world business leaders, including senior executives from the world's top firms such as Alibaba, Tencent, Ford, HSBC and JP Morgan.
It is the fifth time that a Chinese city has hosted the forum. Canadian Prime Minister, Justin Trudeau, and Papua New Guinea's Prime Minister, Peter O'Neill (52), addressed the opening.

7 Dec 2017. Vladimir Putin met in his Novo-Ogaryovo residence with Zhang Youxia, Vice Chairman of the Communist Party of China Central Military Commission and Co-Chairman of the Russian-Chinese Intergovernmental Commission for Military-Technical Cooperation.

7 Dec 2017. Vladimir Putin had a telephone conversation with President Turkey, Recep Tayyip Erdogan, at the initiative of the Turkish side.

Both sides expressed serious concern about the US decision to recognize Jerusalem as Israel's capital, and plans to move the US Embassy there from Tel Aviv. Such steps can thwart all prospects for the Middle East peace process. Further escalation of tensions in the region, it was noted, would be unacceptable. The efforts of the international community should be aimed at facilitating the resumption of Palestinian-Israeli talks in search of a compromise solution to all issues, including the status of Jerusalem.

Russia and Turkey reaffirmed their commitment to achieving a just and viable solution to the Middle East crisis based, above all, on the relevant resolutions of the UN Security Council and the UN General Assembly, as well as the realization of the Palestinian people's right to their own state. Recep Tayyip Erdogan informed President Putin about the calling of an emergency summit of the Organization of Islamic Cooperation (56 member states, with a population of over 1.6 B) devoted to this situation on December 13.

7 Dec 2017. Reports. Large military drills, and U.S. threats of a preemptive strike, have made the outbreak of war on the Korean peninsula "an established fact," according to North Korea's foreign ministry. "The remaining question now is: when will the war break out?" White House national security adviser H.R McMaster said at the weekend the possibility of war with North Korea was "increasing every day."

8 Dec 2017. Xinhua. The Chinese version of the same meeting from above. Russian President Vladimir Putin met a top Chinese military official Thursday, 7 Dec, on improving military cooperation between the two countries. Military cooperation plays an important role in Russia-China relations, and the two countries should continue to strengthen their partnership in joint military drills, army games and personnel training, Putin said.

8 Dec 2017. Reports: China is building space weapons to target U.S. satellites.

9 December 2017. China.org. China to play increasingly crucial role in global governance. The Sanya Forum 2017, a non-

governmental forum for international economic and financial dialogue, opened in Sanya, Hainan Province, on Dec. 9.

With the theme of "Challenges in Global Governance and the Role of China", the two-day event has drawn influential political, business and academic leaders from China, the United States, Europe and the rest of Asia to explore global governance models, and the ways to advance sound development of the world economy. The former French Prime Minister, Dominique de Villepin (64), had the keynote speech at the opening ceremony.

11 Dec 2017. History: On 11 Dec 1972, 45 years ago today, NASA's final Apollo 17 mission landed on the surface of the Moon. No human has walked there since.

Reports: President Trump has signed "Space Policy Directive 1" aimed at returning Americans to the surface of the Moon, and onward to Mars. "Space has so much to do with so many other applications, including a military application," he said.

The White House. Regarding NASA: "Lead an innovative and sustainable program of exploration, with commercial and international partners, to enable human expansion across the solar system, and to bring back to Earth new knowledge and opportunities. Beginning with missions beyond low-Earth orbit, the United States will lead the return of humans to the Moon for long-term exploration and utilization, followed by human missions to Mars and other destinations." On July 20, 1969, American astronaut Neil Armstrong became the first man to walk on the Moon, making "one giant leap for mankind."

·   Apollo 17 was the last manned mission to the Moon, launched 45 years ago on December 7, 1972.

America, the only country to successfully send manned missions to the Moon, has sent 12 astronauts to walk on the Moon.

·   In July 2011, the United States retired the Space Shuttle program, three decades after it began.

From 1981 to 2011, the five Space Shuttles flew 135 missions into space.

·   After the Space Shuttle was retired, the United States has been forced to rely on Russian rockets, at the cost of $70 million per seat.

·   In the coming years the United States will launch astronauts on an American-made rocket and crew system, the Space Launch

System and Orion crew vehicle, and multiple American companies will provide the Pentagon with American engines and rockets to launch national security payloads.

11 Dec 2017. Vladimir Putin arrived on a working visit in Egypt. President of the Arab Republic of Egypt, Abdel Fattah el-Sisi, met Vladimir Putin at the airport.

12 Dec 2017. The White House. United States forces, including strike and combat-support aircraft, and associated United States military personnel, remain deployed to Turkey, at the Turkish government's request, to support Defeat-ISIS operations, and to enhance Turkey's security.

12 Dec 2017. The White House. Consistent with the strategy I (the President) announced publicly on August 21, 2017, United States forces remain in Afghanistan for the purposes of stopping the reemergence of safe havens that enable terrorists to threaten the United States, supporting the Afghan government and the Afghan military, as they confront the Taliban in the field, and creating conditions to support a political process to achieve a lasting peace.

12 Dec 2017. The White House. At the request of the Government of Jordan, approximately 2,300 United States military personnel are deployed to Jordan to support Defeat-ISIS operations, to enhance Jordan's security, and to promote regional stability.

12 Dec 2017. The White House. At the request of the Government of Lebanon, approximately 100 United States military personnel are deployed to Lebanon to enhance the government's counterterrorism capabilities, and to support the Defeat-ISIS operations of Lebanese security forces.

12 Dec 2017. The White House. A small number of United States military personnel are deployed to Yemen to conduct operations against al-Qa'ida in the Arabian Peninsula (AQAP) and ISIS. The United States military continues to work closely with the Government of Yemen, and regional partner forces to dismantle and ultimately eliminate the terrorist threat posed by those groups. Since

the last periodic update report, United States forces have conducted a number of airstrikes against AQAP operatives and facilities in Yemen, and supported the United Arab Emirates- and Yemen-led operations to clear AQAP from Shabwah Governorate. In October, United States forces also conducted airstrikes against ISIS targets in Yemen for the first time. United States forces, in a non-combat role, have also continued to provide logistics and other support to regional forces combatting the Houthi insurgency in Yemen.

12 Dec 2017. The White House. As part of a comprehensive strategy to defeat ISIS, United States Armed Forces are conducting a systematic campaign of airstrikes, and other necessary operations against ISIS forces in Iraq. In Iraq, United States Armed Forces are advising and coordinating with Iraqi forces and providing training, equipment, communications support, intelligence support, and other support to select elements of the Iraqi security forces, including Iraqi Kurdish Peshmerga forces. Actions in Iraq are being undertaken in coordination with the Government of Iraq, and in conjunction with coalition partners.

12 Dec 2017. The White House. As part of a comprehensive strategy to defeat ISIS, United States Armed Forces are conducting a systematic campaign of airstrikes and other necessary operations against ISIS forces in Syria. United States Armed Forces are also conducting airstrikes and other necessary operations against al-Qa'ida in Syria. United States Armed Forces are also deployed to Syria to conduct operations against ISIS with indigenous ground forces. Since the last periodic update report, United States Armed Forces participating in the Defeat-ISIS campaign in Syria have undertaken a limited number of strikes against Syrian government and pro-Syrian government forces. These strikes were lawful measures to counter immediate threats to United States and partner forces engaged in that campaign.

12 Dec 2017. The White House. Approximately 400 United States military personnel are assigned to or supporting the United States contingent of the Multinational Force and Observers, which have been present in Egypt since 1981.

12 Dec 2017. The White House. Additional United States forces are deployed to Kenya, to support counterterrorism operations in East Africa.

12 Dec 2017. The White House. Since the last periodic update report, United States forces have conducted a number of airstrikes against ISIS terrorists and their camps in Libya. These airstrikes were conducted in coordination with Libya's Government of National Accord.

12 Dec 2017. The White House. United States forces continue to partner with the Government of Djibouti, which has permitted use of Djiboutian territory for basing of United States forces. United States military personnel remain deployed to Djibouti, including for purposes of posturing for counterterrorism and counter-piracy operations in the vicinity of the Horn of Africa, and the Arabian Peninsula, and to provide contingency support for embassy security augmentation in East Africa, as required.

12 Dec 2017. The White House. United States forces continue to counter the terrorist threat posed by ISIS and al-Shabaab, an associated force of al-Qa'ida. Since the last periodic report, United States forces have conducted a limited number of airstrikes against al-Shabaab as well as ISIS. United States forces also advise, assist, and accompany regional forces, including Somali and African Union Mission in Somalia (AMISOM) forces, during counterterrorism operations.

12 Dec 2017. The White House. On October 4, 2017, an element, assessed to be part of ISIS, attacked United States and Nigerien forces in Niger. The attack resulted in the deaths of four United States service members. Approximately 800 United States military personnel remain deployed to Niger.

12 Dec 2017. The White House. United States military personnel are also deployed to Nigeria to support counterterrorism operations.

12 Dec 2017. The White House. United States military personnel are also deployed to Cameroon to support counterterrorism operations.

12 Dec 2017. The White House. United States military personnel in the Lake Chad Basin and Sahel Region continue to conduct airborne intelligence, surveillance, and reconnaissance operations, and to provide support to African and European partners conducting counterterrorism operations in the region, including by advising, assisting, and accompanying these partner forces. United States military personnel are also deployed to Chad to support counterterrorism operations.

12 Dec 2017. Ankara. The Russian head of state and Turkish President Recep Tayyip Erdogan discussed current issues of bilateral cooperation, primarily the progress of implementing major joint energy projects. They also exchanged views on key international issues, including the situation in the Middle East and the Syrian settlement process. Earlier on the same day, Vladimir Putin visited the Khmeimim Air Base in Syria, and Egypt.
Erdogan: The decision by the US leadership to recognize Jerusalem as the capital of Israel resulted in major unrest. This was a disappointment for Muslims, Christians, and for the reasonable Jewish population. By the end of last week, four Palestinians were killed, and about 2,000 wounded by Israeli soldiers. Israeli aircraft bombed the Gaza Strip.

13 Dec 2017. The White House. The National Defense Authorization Act for fiscal year 2018, approves one of the largest defense spending increases since the Reagan presidency, to help rebuild America's Armed Forces.
Here is a quick list of what the NDAA does for America's military:
Increases, rather than shrinks, the size of our forces for the first time in 7 years
Ensures that our military remains the world's preeminent fighting force, which is vital to the Administration's peace-through-strength strategy

Authorizes funding to allow for the continued defeat of ISIS, and cover critical missile defense capabilities, to confront the threat posed by North Korea

Takes concrete steps to rebuild U.S. military readiness

Approves a 2.4% pay raise for our troops—the largest in 8 years.

Reports about the cost: FY 2018 defense budget promises a "historic" defense buildup. At $603 billions in the base national defense budget, $54 billions are over the Budget Control Act caps. The $4.1 trillions budget has a deficit of over $440 billions.

The US National debt is over $24 T, and growing faster than ever.

The arms race heats up, and everybody loses.

14 Dec 2017. Reports: Looking to get relations back on track, South Korean President Moon Jae-in will meet Chinese President Xi Jinping today, 14 Dec, after a year-long standoff over the deployment the U.S. THAAD system. Curbing North Korea's nuclear ambitions will top the agenda, while the two leaders will sign an MOU on restarting negotiations to further open China's service and investment sectors to South Korea companies.

14 Dec 2017, 5:15 PM. The White House. President Donald J. Trump (71.5) spoke with President Vladimir Putin (65.1) of Russia today. President Trump thanked President Putin for acknowledging America's strong economic performance in his annual press conference. The two presidents also discussed working together to resolve the very dangerous situation in North Korea.

15 Dec 2017, 1:15 AM. The Kremlin. Vladimir Putin had a telephone conversation with US President Donald Trump at the initiative of the American side. The two leaders discussed current issues on the bilateral agenda, as well as the situation in crisis areas in the world, primarily the Korean nuclear issue.

They have agreed to maintain contact.

15 Dec 2017. Xinhua. President Xi Jinping has urged the People's Liberation Army to restructure and enhance its combat capability. Xi, also general secretary of the Communist Party of China Central Committee, and chairman of the Central Military

Commission, was speaking during an inspection on Wednesday, 13 Dec, of the 71st Group Army of the PLA. Xi told officers that they should grasp the spirit of the 19th CPC National Congress, and incorporate those principles into military practice.

15 Dec 2017. Reports: Russia is not ready to sign up to new sanctions on North Korea that would strangle the isolated country economically, according to Deputy Foreign Minister, Igor Morgulov.

16 Dec 2017. Xinhua. President Xi Jinping on Friday, 16 Dec, reaffirmed the central government's long-term and unswerving adherence to the principle of "one country, two systems" in Hong Kong and Macao, when he met with the chief executives of the two special administrative regions (SARs). Xi also said the report of the 19th CPC National Congress had proposed to integrate Hong Kong's and Macao's development into the overall development of the country.

17 Dec 2017, 11:40 AM. The White House. President Vladimir V. Putin of Russia called President Donald J. Trump today to thank him for the advanced warning the United States intelligence agencies provided to Russia, concerning a major terror plot in Saint Petersburg, Russia. Based on the information the United States provided, Russian authorities were able to capture the terrorists just prior to an attack that could have killed large numbers of people. No Russian lives were lost, and the terrorist attackers were caught and are now incarcerated. President Trump appreciated the call, and told President Putin that he and the entire United States intelligence community were pleased to have helped save so many lives. President Trump stressed the importance of intelligence cooperation to defeat terrorists wherever they may be. Both leaders agreed that this serves as an example of the positive things that can occur when our countries work together. President Putin extended his thanks and congratulations to Central Intelligence Agency (CIA) Director Mike Pompeo and the CIA. President Trump then called Director Pompeo to congratulate him, his very talented people, and the entire intelligence community on a job well done!

17 Dec 2017, 7:40 PM. The Kremlin. Vladimir Putin had a telephone conversation with President of the United States Donald Trump. Vladimir Putin thanked Donald Trump for the information passed on by the United States' Central Intelligence Agency (CIA) that helped detain the terrorists, who plotted to set off explosions at Kazan Cathedral in St Petersburg, and other public places in the city. The information received from the CIA was enough to locate and detain the criminals. The Russian President asked the US President to convey his appreciation to the Central Intelligence Agency director, and the operatives of US intelligence services, who received this information.

Vladimir Putin assured Donald Trump that in the event that Russian intelligence services receive information that concerns terrorist threats to the US and its citizens, they will promptly pass it on to their US colleagues via partner channels.

19 Dec 2017. The White House. President Donald J. Trump spoke today with Prime Minister Theresa May of the United Kingdom. The two leaders exchanged holiday greetings and warm wishes for Christmas and the New Year. The Prime Minister offered her condolences for the tragic train accident in Washington State.

19 Dec 2017. Vladimir Putin held talks in the Kremlin with President of Serbia, Aleksandar Vucic, who is in Russia on a working visit.

19 Dec 2017. The White House. President Donald J. Trump spoke today with President Shavkat Mirziyoyev of Uzbekistan to discuss regional security, and to explore opportunities for improved cooperation.

20 Dec 2017. The White House. President Donald J. Trump spoke today with King Salman bin Abdulaziz Al Saud of Saudi Arabia.

20 Dec 2017. Reports: Beijing restored a ban on mainland tour groups traveling to South Korea. The ban comes just over a month before the 2018 Pyeongchang Winter Olympics being hosted by Seoul.

21 Dec 2017. Reports: President Trump has threatened to cut off financial aid to countries that vote in favor of a draft UN resolution, calling for the U.S. to withdraw its decision to recognize Jerusalem as Israel's capital. "They take hundreds of millions of dollars, and even billions of dollars, and then they vote against us. Well, we're watching those votes. We'll save a lot."

21 Dec 2017. Vladimir Putin had a telephone conversation with acting Chancellor of Germany, Angela Merkel, at the initiative of the German side. (President Macron of France is 40 today).
While discussing the crisis situation in southeastern Ukraine, Angela Merkel was interested to know the reasons for the withdrawal of Russian army officers from the Joint Centre for Control and Coordination of the Ceasefire and Stabilization of the Line of the Contact between the Sides (JCCC).
Vladimir Putin noted in particular that for a long time the Ukrainian authorities have been purposely complicating the presence of Russian officers, and the performance of their duties, through various restrictions and provocations. There has been no response to Russia's repeated proposals to deal with the unacceptable situation that has evolved. The Russian and German leaders agreed to continue the discussion of outstanding issues that must be resolved in order for the JCCC to resume full-fledged operation. They agreed that their aides would continue to work on conditions that would make it possible for Russian officers to return to the center.
In addition, Vladimir Putin and Angela Merkel spoke in favor of implementing the initiative to exchange persons held by the parties to the domestic Ukrainian conflict as soon as possible, and supported the Christmas armistice declared by the Contact Group.

22 Dec 2017. Xinhua. Chinese President Xi Jinping on Thursday, 21 Dec, underscored the one-China principle, as he hosted Gambian President, Adama Barrow (52), on his first China visit, since diplomatic relations were resumed last year.

22 Dec 2017. Vladimir Putin had a telephone conversation with President of Turkey, Recep Tayyip Erdogan.

The two presidents discussed the situation in the Middle East, in the context of the UN General Assembly resolution on the status of Jerusalem. They reaffirmed their countries' resolve to continue to promote a Palestinian-Israeli settlement based on international law, and the right of the Palestinian people to have an independent state of their own.

22 Dec 2017. Reports: After threatening to cut off financial aid, 128 countries defied President Trump on Thursday, 21 Dec, and voted in favor of a UN resolution calling for the U.S. to drop its recent recognition of Jerusalem as Israel's capital. According to figures from USAID, the U.S. provided some $38 B in economic and military assistance to foreign countries in 2016.

22 Dec 2017. Reports: Russian Defense Minister, Sergei Shoigu, said at a meeting that the budget of Russia's defense spending in 2018 will decrease to 46 billions of U.S. dollars (less than 7% of the US defense budget, which is larger than the next 9 countries combined (China, Saudi Arabia, Russia, UK, India, France, Japan, Germany and South Korea).

25 Dec 2017. Vladimir Putin had a telephone conversation with President of Turkmenistan, Gurbanguly Berdimuhamedov, on the initiative of the Turkmen side.

27 Dec 2017. An informal meeting of the heads of CIS states was held at the Russian presidential residence in Novo-Ogaryovo. The meeting was attended by President of the Republic of Azerbaijan Ilham Aliyev President of the Republic of Armenia Serzh Sargsyan, President of the Republic of Belarus Alexander Lukashenko, President of the Republic of Kazakhstan Nursultan Nazarbayev, President of the Republic of Kyrgyzstan Sooronbay Jeenbekov, President of the Republic of Moldova Igor Dodon, President of the Republic of Tajikistan Emomali Rahmon and President of the Republic of Uzbekistan, Shavkat Mirziyoyev
The leaders of the CIS countries summed up the results of Russia's CIS Presidency in 2017 and exchanged views on the further development of cooperation in different areas. On January 1, 2018, Russia will transfer its CIS Presidency to Tajikistan.

27 Dec 2017. Vladimir Putin had a meeting in Russia with President of the Republic of Kazakhstan, Nursultan Nazarbayev.

27 Dec 2017. Vladimir Putin had a brief bilateral meeting with President of Moldova, Igor Dodon, on the sidelines of the informal summit in Russia.

27 Dec 2017. Reports: China's ruling Communist Party will meet next month to discuss amending the constitution for the first time since 2004, the Xinhua News Agency reports. Speculation has increased that Xi Jinping might seek to stay in office beyond 2022, after unveiling a leadership lineup in October that didn't include a potential heir. Under the current constitution, the president can only serve two five-year terms.

Reports: In China, Google's search engine has been blocked by censorship authorities since 2012.

28 Dec 2017. The White House. The United States strongly condemns today's barbaric attack at a cultural and social center in Kabul, Afghanistan, and offers its deepest condolences to the victims and their families.

28 Dec 2017. Reports: The blast that ripped through a Christmas market in St. Petersburg yesterday, 27 Dec, was a "terrorist act," according to Russian President Vladimir Putin. The explosion injured at least 13 shoppers, although no group has yet claimed responsibility.

29 Dec 2017. The White House. President Donald J. Trump spoke today with President Abdel Fattah Al Sisi of Egypt to offer condolences to the people of Egypt, after the attack on worshippers and security forces in the city of Helwan, which is located south of Cairo.

29 Dec 2017. Reports: "Caught red handed - very disappointed that China is allowing oil to go into North Korea," President Trump wrote in a tweet. Ship-to-ship trading of goods

between the nations had been specifically banned in September's UN resolution. "If they don't help us with North Korea, then I do what I've always said I want to do," he told the NYT, threatening to take trade measures against China.

30 Dec 2017. In his message of greetings to President of the United States of America, Donald Trump (71.5), Mr. Putin (65.2) noted, among other things, his strong belief that in the current challenging international environment, it is especially important for Russia and the US to engage in constructive dialogue, with a view to enhancing global strategic stability, and finding the best solutions to the global challenges and threats. The President of Russia stressed the importance of the principles of equality and mutual respect as the foundation for developing bilateral relations. "This would allow us to make progress in promoting pragmatic cooperation, designed for the long term," the message reads.

30 Dec 2017. In his greetings to President of China, Xi Jinping (64.5), on the New Year and upcoming Spring Festival, the Russian President noted that 2017 has brought more success in Russian-Chinese relations, with substantial growth in mutual trade and dynamic exchanges in science and technology, and culture and the humanitarian sphere. Vladimir Putin emphasized the fact that Moscow and Beijing cooperate extensively in global affairs and contribute greatly to the solutions of current international problems.

30 Dec 2017. Vladimir Putin sent holiday greetings to French President, Emmanuel Macron (40): "Our meeting in Versailles and telephone contacts have allowed us to discuss many current issues of bilateral relations and key international issues at length. I expect to continue our constructive dialogue and joint work aimed at strengthening Russian-French links. I look forward to your visit to Russia," the message reads.

30 Dec 2017. In his greetings to Prime Minister of Japan, Shinzo Abe (63.3), the President of Russia noted with satisfaction that recently, Russian-Japanese relations had progressed in a number of key areas. Thus, the political dialogue has intensified,

with foreign and defense ministers' consultations resuming in the 'two plus two' format, and inter-parliamentary links have expanded.

30 Dec 2017. Vladimir Putin has had a telephone conversation with President of Finland, Sauli Niinisto (69.3).
The leaders exchanged warm New Year's greetings, and extended their best wishes to the people of both nations.

Children, who routinely eat their meals together with their family, are more likely to experience long-term physical and mental health benefits, a new Canadian study shows. – Universite de Montreal, Journal of Developmental & Behavioural Paediatrics, December 2017.

11 July 2009, from the Northern Avenue, near Seaport Hotel & World Trade Center, looking northeast to tall ships anchored at Boston Fish Pier (the oldest continuously operated fish pier in US).